MUSCLE MECHANICS

Everett Aaberg

Director of Education and Personal Training
International Athletic Club Management
Dallas, Texas

Human Kinetics

Library of Congress Cataloging-in-Publication Data

Aaberg, Everett, 1963-
    Muscle mechanics / Everett Aaberg.
       p.   cm.
    "This book is a revised edition of Bio-mechanically correct,
published in 1996 by Realistic Individualized Professional Services,
Dallas"--T.p. verso.
    Includes bibliographical references and index.
    ISBN 0-88011-796-6 (pbk.)
    1. Weight training. 2. Exercise.   I. Aaberg, Everett, 1963-
Bio-mechanically correct.   II Title.
GV546.A23   1998
613.7'1--dc21   98-13154
                                           CIP

ISBN: 0-88011-796-6

This book is a revised edition of *Bio-Mechanically Correct*, published in 1996 by Realistic Individualized Professional Training Services, Dallas.

Acquisitions Editor: Martin Barnard; **Developmental Editor:** Kristine Enderle; **Assistant Editor:** Laura Hambly; **Copyeditor:** Michele Sandifer; **Proofreader:** Jim Burns; **Indexer:** Joan Griffitts; **Graphic Designer:** Nancy Rasmus; **Graphic Artist:** Denise Lowry; **Photo Editor:** Boyd Lafoon; **Cover Designer:** Jack Davis; **Photographer:** Tom Roberts; **Illustrator:** Scott Beckley; **Printer:** VG Reed

Human Kinetics books are available at special discounts for bulk purchase. Special editions or book excerpts can also be created to specification. For details, contact the Special Sales Manager at Human Kinetics.

Printed in the United States of America   10   9   8   7   6   5   4   3   2   1

Human Kinetics
Web site: http://www.humankinetics.com/

United States: Human Kinetics, P.O. Box 5076, Champaign, IL 61825-5076
1-800-747-4457
e-mail: humank@hkusa.com

Canada: Human Kinetics, 475 Devonshire Road Unit 100, Windsor, ON N8Y 2L5
1-800-465-7301
e-mail: humank@hkcanada.com

Europe: Human Kinetics, P.O. Box IW14, Leeds LS16 6TR, United Kingdom
(44) 1132 781708
e-mail: humank@hkeurope.com

Australia: Human Kinetics, 57A Price Avenue, Lower Mitcham, South Australia 5062
(088) 277 1555
e-mail: humank@hkaustralia.com

New Zealand: Human Kinetics, P.O. Box 105-231, Auckland 1
(09) 523 3462
e-mail: humank@hknewz.com

CONTENTS

PREFACE

This book is designed to update you on the newest advances and changes pertaining to resistance training. It will provide you with the safest and most efficient collection of resistance-training exercises and techniques based on the best scientific information available today.

This book is not intended to teach in-depth anatomy, kinesiology, or biomechanics. Rather, the goal is to teach the most efficient and safest resistance-training techniques developed while considering and applying a combination of all of these fields of study. This book will, however, provide you with basic information about the human body's bones, joints, and muscles. You will learn how the interaction of these systems allows for the various types of movements that can be performed by the human body.

Knowing how and what makes the body move is important when learning new resistance-training techniques. After all, resistance training, simply stated, is the movement or attempted movement of the body against a given resistance. The more knowledge you have of the human body's design and movement capabilities, the better you will comprehend the philosophy and reasoning behind the training techniques presented herein.

Prior hands-on experience with resistance training may be very helpful but is not necessary. In fact, in many cases, a person's prior experience may prove to be more of a hindrance than a help, depending on where that experience came from and the person's attachment to it.

Throughout our lives, most of us have learned certain things which we may have developed very strong feelings and opinions about. Eventually, these beliefs are challenged, and we are forced to question them. Fitness is still a relatively young field of study. We should look on any new ideas presented with an open mind and perhaps analyze the validity of our present beliefs. Many times, if we trace them to their origins, we will find that our present beliefs have been passed on to us from less-than-reliable sources. This is particularly true about resistance training.

Most of us have learned resistance training in gyms or weight rooms and not in the classroom. Our instructors were not exercise physiologists, kinesiologists, or fitness professionals. Instead, they were coaches, peers, or some abnormally muscular person who we felt must be knowledgeable because of his or her appearance. We now know that genetics plays a large role in one's muscularity. In many cases, these extremely muscular individuals receive great results despite how they train rather than because of the manner in which they train. Chances are that most of these well-meaning people were simply passing on information that they had learned from a similar source—information that had very little scientific basis behind it. Typically, they were not being negligent. Very little information and research were available about resistance training at the time. Unfortunately, even though information is now beginning to surface, many people have not accessed the proper resources and are continuing to train and instruct many outdated techniques.

Muscle Mechanics has taken many traditional resistance- and weight-training exercises and applied to them the sciences of anatomy, kinesiology, physiology and most of all, biomechanics. All of the exercises have been analyzed for their efficiency and safety. How these exercises affect the joints, the connective tissues, and the entire body, as well as the muscles they were designed to develop, were studied. For many traditional exercises, certain modifications have been made on such things as alignment, positioning, range of motion, and technique. Other exercises were judged ineffective, compromised the safety of the body, or in some instances, did both. In these cases, "why shouldn't" these exercises continue to be taught was not asked. Rather, "why should" they continue to be taught was asked. I see no need for people to perform high-risk exercises when safer alternatives are available.

This book presents 73 different exercises plus some variations. These are by no means the only safe and effective exercises possible. Rather, consider these exercises as a great base or foundation from which you can learn and add to as you continue toward your fitness goals. The exercises and techniques presented in this book have been developed, analyzed, and approved by some of the top exercise physiologists, physical therapists, doctors, and personal trainers in the country.

Approach this book with an open mind and confidence in its information. I believe you will experience a higher degree of safety and will greatly enhance the efficiency of your training as you implement these exercises into your personal fitness program or those of your clients and athletes.

ACKNOWLEDGMENTS

No book is ever just the work of one individual. Besides all of the people who have directly contributed to the final production, a multitude of individuals have helped, influenced, and contributed in a more indirect manner as well. My involvement in the fitness industry over the last 15 years has allowed me to learn from numerous teachers, fitness experts, medical and health care professionals, colleagues, peers, and friends. They all have helped me along the way and added to my continuing education and experience. So many people have taught and helped me that I cannot even begin to mention them all. However, I would especially like to thank some of the following individuals or groups.

I would like to thank Dr. Kenneth Cooper and the entire staff of the Cooper Fitness Center where my work on this book began. You all deserve your reputation of being world-class leaders.

I would like to thank Dr. Sterling, Susan Johnson, and the entire staff at the Cooper Institute of Aerobic Research for also being world-class leaders in research and in providing continuing education. I am honored and grateful to have been given the opportunity to work with all of you in further educating fitness professionals.

As I mentioned, I have been influenced and helped by a multitude of people over the past several years but none more than by Tom Purvis. His lectures, videotapes, and personal conversations have done more to shape my views about fitness, biomechanics, and resistance training than anyone thus far in my career. Tom, Mitch Simon, and their company, Focus on Fitness, are truly on the cutting edge of the fitness industry.

All of the illustrations and artwork were done by artist, and personal friend of mine since high school, Scott Beckley of Beckley Illustrations. I know and appreciate the extra time and care that he dedicated to this project.

A very special thanks to Human Kinetics. You are the world leader in health and fitness publications, and I am honored to have my book published and distributed through you.

INTRODUCTION

Resistance training is fast becoming the most popular and highest demanded exercise in the world today. Although some people who exercise on a regular basis choose to engage only in aerobic activities such as running, bicycling, cardiovascular machines, and aerobics classes, many more are adding or substituting resistance training for some of their aerobic workouts. Why? Simply put, resistance training provides several benefits that aerobic exercise cannot. It may be the single most important activity people can perform to preserve and improve their quality of life. Nothing can strengthen the muscles, joints, and bones like resistance training—thus making any activity easier, more enjoyable, and safer.

Besides providing strengthening benefits, resistance training has many applications in the rehabilitation and prevention of injuries. Resistance training can also be used to help correct musculature imbalances that can cause structural alignment problems such as poor posture and deviated curvatures of the spine.

Resistance training can even play a part in battling certain diseases such as diabetes, arthritis, high blood pressure, and heart disease. It is also, by far, the best form of exercise to treat and prevent osteoporosis, because resistance training helps increase the body's bone density.

As we age, the effects of gravity become more and more apparent. It is visible in our posture, our gait, and the overall way in which we move and function. A good resistance-training program, carried on throughout our lives, can make a remarkable difference in how we are affected by this phenomenon.

Cosmetically, resistance training builds, shapes, and even sculpts the human body like nothing else. It develops the muscles that give shape to the body. In addition, due to the metabolic increase associated with gaining lean tissue, resistance training is also a key factor in reducing body fat.

Resistance training complements aerobic activities. Aerobic activity has been proven and well documented for its cardiovascular and numerous other health benefits. Therefore, we should all do a combination of both resistance training and cardiovascular work to achieve optimum health. (Together they will not only increase longevity, but dramatically improve the quality of life.)

To be of benefit, however, resistance training must be done correctly. Done improperly, it may offer little or no benefit and, in many cases, can cause more harm than good. Several types, forms, and techniques of resistance training are utilized for different purposes. Each is designed to accomplish different goals. As discussed in the preface, some traditional exercises may be outdated, inconsistent with your goals, or inappropriate for you and your body.

The primary goal and design of this book are to teach you the safest and most efficient methods of moving and stabilizing your body against a resistance. You will be provided with numerous resistance-training exercises and techniques presented in an easy-to-follow, step-by-step process that are all biomechanically correct. Several exercises are included for each region and for every major muscle group of the body.

This book will also provide an introduction about how to select and combine exercises in a proper balance and sequence that will develop a base program appropriate for you. This will start you off safely on the road toward your personal fitness goals. You will also learn how to determine the sets, repetitions, and approximate amount of resistance you should use. These are all elements of a good program design.

Program design is a topic in itself and could easily take at least an entire book or even a series of books to cover all the aspects involved. If you are not a fitness professional, I suggest that you consult with one to help you design your program. Be sure the person is certified and preferably has a degree in the fitness field. He or she should be able to instruct you properly about performing the exercises provided in this book and competently explain any of the information presented herein.

It is also always a good idea to see a physician before beginning any exercise program. If you have any illness, disease, injury, joint problem, or other pre–existing condition, some of these exercises or techniques may not be appropriate. Please, ask your doctor first.

CHAPTER 1

THE PRINCIPLES OF MUSCLE MECHANICS

This book will present and attempt to teach you unique resistance-training exercises and techniques rather than typical weightlifting ones. In weightlifting, the goal is to lift or move weight. Therefore, your technique is designed to accomplish that goal. Your entire thought process before and during the weightlifting exercise focuses on the goal of moving the weight.

Resistance Training Versus Weightlifting

During resistance training, your goal is to move muscle, not weight. Therefore, you should approach each exercise with an entirely different thought process and use a completely different technique. You should attempt to focus solely on your body, on its position throughout the exercise, and on the muscles you are contracting. You should direct very little of your concentration on the weight, bar, or machine. By having different goals and mastering different techniques, you will obtain different results. The results you will experience are far superior to that of just being able to move more weight. To help you further understand the difference, I have referenced *Merriam Webster's Collegiate Dictionary* for the following definitions.

- Weight—the heaviness of a thing when weighed or the amount that something weighs
- Lift—to raise or to exert oneself in raising something

So in other words, by weightlifting, people learn how to lift heavy things.

As previously stated, we have a completely different goal with resistance training. Again, I will consult *Merriam Webster's Collegiate Dictionary* for the following definitions.

- Resistance—to strive against or to oppose with success
- Training—to educate or discipline, undergo systematic exercise or preparation

So by applying these definitions we could say that with resistance training, people learn how to successfully oppose an outside force through systematic exercise that prepares, disciplines, and educates their bodies.

With this in mind, people do not learn how to push dumbbells, pull bars, or lift weights with resistance training. Instead, they learn how to position and stabilize their bodies as they control and focus on contracting muscles and moving bones.

By focusing more on the body than on the resistance, not only do people work the targeted muscles more efficiently, but they are also less likely to become injured. During most exercises, the muscles are learning to stabilize the body while in proper spinal alignment, which will help provide better posture. These are some benefits of using what I call a *wholistic* approach to resistance training.

I would describe this wholistic approach to resistance training as one that focuses on the entire body and pays particular attention to the body's alignment, positioning, and desired motion. This maximizes benefits while reducing the risk involved in each exercise. (See figure 1.1.)

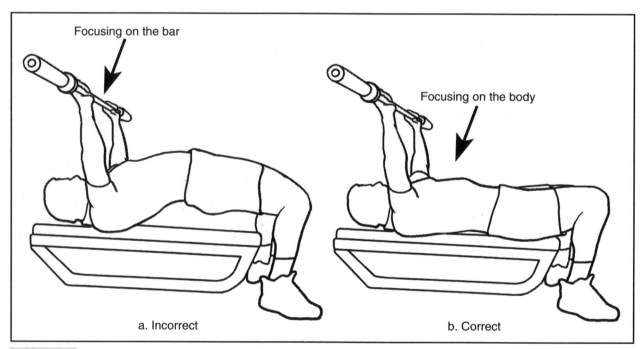

Focusing on the bar

Focusing on the body

a. Incorrect

b. Correct

Figure 1.1 Chest press

The Results and Benefits

According to the American Council on Exercise, approximately 50 percent of the American population do any activity at all. What is more depressing is that only about 22 percent of those people are actually receiving any noticeable benefits from their exercise programs. In most cases, these low success rates are probably not due to the programs themselves but rather result from how the programs are being performed.

I believe that by using and mastering a wholistic approach to resistance training, you will receive more benefits than do individuals who just lift weights. Let's look at a few of these benefits in more detail.

Greater Efficiency for the Targeted Muscles

Focus on the actual joint motions you are performing during the exercise, and concentrate on the specific muscles responsible for activating the motion. These techniques decrease the body's urge to involve other muscle groups, thus placing a greater stress on the primary movers.

Reduced Risk of Injury

By strictly holding the entire body's position while keeping the spine stable during the exercise, the risk of injury is dramatically reduced. Safety is always a major concern during resistance training and is ultimately the responsibility of the individual performing the exercise. The machine, the equipment, or even a trainer cannot completely ensure your safety. You must learn how to position and align your own body when an outside force opposes it. This will also help you feel how best to position, stabilize, and move your body against resistance that occurs outside the gym during your daily activities.

Better Posture

Teaching the body to hold proper positioning and posture in the presence of an outside force is the key to preparing the body functionally for everyday activities and for life in general. Many of the movements performed in a resistance-training program are never repeated anywhere during real life activities. However, the standing and seated positions you train in often occur in real life. As you consistently practice these positions properly during your resistance-training program in the gym, your body will become significantly stronger while in these positions. As a result, you will be noticeably more comfortable and having to sit or stand for long periods of time will feel less stressful. These increases in balance, posture, and stability may be more important and of greater benefit to many individuals than the increases in strength and power also experienced by following this wholistic approach to resistance training.

Consistency

I have found that the individuals who have taken the time to learn to train properly stay more motivated and have a much higher adherence to their programs. They may have much clearer and better-defined goals and expectations of their fitness programs than do people who have not learned to train properly. They also usually experience less injuries, both in and out of the gym. Many times, injuries force people to stop training altogether or at least temporarily. Perhaps some people train more consistently simply because they have experienced better results by using these methods. Whatever the reason or combination of reasons, I find that people who have learned to train properly are more consistent and persistent, which are two key elements for success.

Combine these advantages with all the other benefits that proper resistance training offers (as mentioned in the introduction). You can easily see how training properly by using *Muscle Mechanics* could be the most important thing you've ever done for the integrity of your body.

Types of Resistance

To perform resistance training, there must first be a resistance. Most often when people think about resistance training, they automatically think of weights. Some may visualize dumbbells, barbells, and metal plates. Others may think more of pulleys, cables, and machines. Though different, these are all weights with gravity providing the actual resistance. Weights are the most commonly used type of resistance and are predominantly what we use in this book. However, it is important to realize that other types of resistance can be effectively used in place of weights or in conjunction with them. Learning these alternatives will provide you with a wider scope of training exercises and add variety to your fitness program. The following paragraphs summarize some of the different types of resistance.

Isometric Resistance

An isometric contraction is one in which the contracting forces of the muscles are equal to that of the resistance. Therefore, the muscle neither shortens nor lengthens. Isometric resistance can come from a variety of sources. For instance, an immovable object such as a wall or a heavy piece of equipment can be used to create an isometric contraction of the muscles. Isometric resistance can be created independently by pressing the hands together with equal force, for example. Isometric resistance can also be provided by another person. For example, trainers may have clients sit in a "ready position" on a bench or a Resista-Ball. The client tries to hold that position as the trainer applies pressure from different angles. This isometric type of training can help to develop increased spinal stability. Isometric training has also proven very effective for gaining strength. However, it only strengthens the muscles at the particular point where the isometric contraction takes place.

Dynamic Constant Resistance

In this type of training, the resistance used is constant. The most common examples of this would be free weights and certain machines that use only round pulleys or rollers to redirect the resistance, but they do not alter the resistance during exercise.

Dynamic Variable Resistance

This type of training uses a resistance that is altered or varied during the exercise. Typically, training is done on a weight machine that uses some type of cam. Many types of weight equipment on the market today are of this design. These machines attempt to match the mechanics of the human body by increasing or decreasing the resistance to match the strengths and weaknesses of the body as it performs the exercise. Since the human body is such a complex piece of equipment, very few machines have effectively imitated it.

Dynamic Progressive Resistance

This type of resistance increases as the movement of the body continues through the exercise. Elastic tubing, rubber bands, and springs are examples of this type of resistance. Training with these types of equipment has its benefits, such as cost and convenience, and can be a great tool if applied properly.

Isokinetic Resistance

Isokinetics refers to the contraction of a muscle performed at a constant angular velocity. This means that the speed at which the muscle lengthens and shortens is constant, but not necessarily the resistance. The motion cannot be accelerated. Any force applied in an attempt to increase velocity results in an equal reaction force. These opposing forces will mirror each other throughout the range of motion. Machines of this type usually use hydraulic shock absorbers to provide the resistance. Skilled trainers can provide a similar resistance with their own hands or bodies.

There are also methods available that combine resistance types. For example you can use a technique in which you pause and isometrically squeeze the muscle at the end or peak contraction of the lift. As you progress through the exercise, this end or peak point will vary due to the muscles' ability to complete the original range of motion. In this case, you would obtain the benefit of isometric training at several different points while still performing a dynamic type exercise. (See chapter 5, the Technique sections.)

Other types of resistance equipment use clutches, friction, or electronic devices with motors and pumps. Whatever they use for the actual resistance, this equipment still provides types of resistance similar to those previously described. Remember, whatever type of equipment you use, the focus during resistance training is still on moving your muscles—not on moving the weight or the resistance.

Naming of Exercise

During the process of writing this book and researching the exercises included, I found a general lack of consistency in the way exercises have been taught and presented over the years. No real method or science exists even to name the exercises. Some exercises (and weight machines, for that matter) were named technically, such as *knee extension,* while others appear to have been made up by someone according to what the exercise looked like it was doing, such as *leg curl*. Several exercises have numerous titles for them, like the lateral raise, which is also known as a shoulder raise, dumbbell side raise, medial deltoid fly, or any combination of these names. For anyone who has been around the gym or been training long enough, these multiple names may be only a little confusing. For those people who aren't in the fitness industry or who don't hang out at the club every day, this lack of standardized names can become extremely frustrating. For consistency, the exercises will be listed by using the following method.

For all single-joint motion exercises, we will use the following method:

- First by the type of resistance being used, such as dumbbell, barbell, cable, or machine.
- Second by the main muscle being targeted, such as the chest, biceps, hamstring, or lats (short for latissimus dorsi). Due to several combinations of muscles used for trunk and hip joint motions, exercises that target these areas will be referred to simply as trunk or hip exercises.
- Last by the joint motion being conducted, such as flexion, extension, abduction, adduction, or rotation.

For example, what many people call a dumbbell arm curl shall be listed as a dumbbell biceps flexion or dumbbell biceps flex.

For all compound or multiple-joint motions, we will use the following method:

- First by the type of resistance being used, such as dumbbell, barbell, cable, or machine.
- Second by the main muscle being targeted, such as the chest, lats, back, trunk, or legs.
- Last by the action produced from the combination of joint motions, such as a press, pull down, row, squat, or lunge.

For example, the traditional bench press will be referred to as a barbell chest press.

This is a simple method to adopt that brings consistency and standardization to resistance training. Someone can learn the word *flex* as easily as the word *curl*. Training should be educational as well as physical. By using names of exercises that link the muscles to the joint motions they produce, you will learn something about your body just by knowing the name of the exercise. Keep in mind they are just names. If you know an exercise by another name and feel more comfortable referring to it as such, then by all means do so. It is much more important how the exercise is performed than what it is called.

Determine Your Goals

For whatever reason you are interested in resistance training, one thing is certain—you must already have some goal in mind. If you didn't, you wouldn't be reading this book. Perhaps you are looking to further your education, expand your experience, or enhance your training skills. Maybe you are someone trying to learn what resistance training is about or how you can best get started. Whatever the reason, try to take a moment to clearly determine what your personal fitness goals are. Everyone should have some goals concerning their health and their bodies. I would like you to stop, take a few minutes, and write down yours.

It is important to know what you are trying to accomplish with resistance training before you begin. These overall goals should determine which exercises you choose and the intensity, volume, duration, and frequency at which you perform them. Remember, goals are not achieved overnight. You must have persistence in order to experience success.

Learn the Technique

Learn and perform the steps of technique for every resistance exercise you do. Even if you have someone training or assisting you with such things as alignment, positioning, and range of motion, you will benefit from learning these specifics yourself. Remember, you are ultimately responsible for your own body. This information is provided in chapter 4 in the section about technique.

Know Your Limits

This means finding out exactly what you are now capable of doing and what you cannot do. Resistance training is designed to be challenging. Your training should safely test your limits yet should not push you into high levels of risk.

Communication

If you have a trainer, even for just one set, it is important to let that person know any concerns you may have regarding that particular exercise and the expectations you have of that trainer while he or she assists you. If you have a permanent trainer or partner, it is good to communicate about the actual feelings your body is experiencing during or as a result of the exercise. Remember, you are the only one that really knows how an exercise feels to you.

Working With a Trainer

Muscle Mechanics is in a format to serve as your own personal trainer and to empower you to begin resistance training safely and efficiently on your own. However, to further increase your percentages for success and maximize your results, you may want to consider working with a personal trainer.

The use of personal trainers is becoming more and more common. Several years ago, primarily only affluent people, competitive athletes, or individuals with special needs utilized personal trainers. Now many people of all walks of life realize the benefit of working with a fitness professional. They are finding out how much greater their chance is to reach their goals when they are directed, instructed, coached, and monitored by someone whose sole purpose is to help people get fit.

For many people, using a trainer full-time may not be necessary or affordable. For these people, I suggest at least monthly training sessions, if possible, to measure progress, re-establish new goals, check form, and occasionally redesign the workout plan.

When attempting to select a trainer, be sure he or she is certified by a nationally recognized organization, preferably has a degree in the health sciences, is insured, has current CPR training, has experience, and can provide several references. Try to watch him or her in action prior to hiring in order to see the trainer's style and attentiveness to the client's form. Look around before choosing, and talk with past and present clients for their impressions of the trainer. Also, be sure that the trainer you interview is familiar with the advanced techniques and exercise specifics presented in this book.

CHAPTER 2

BASIC MUSCLE ANATOMY

The musculoskeletal system consists of three separate yet very interdependent components.

- The bones (skeleton)
- The joints
- The muscles

Any movement characteristic of the human body depends on the interaction of these three systems. Muscles do not directly exert force against the ground or an external object. Therefore, muscles do not actually move objects or weights. Instead, they function by moving the bones that rotate about the connective joints. These internal movements transfer a force through the body to the external object or resistance, thus causing the object or resistance to move.

It is impossible for muscles to push. They can only pull. As the muscles pull the bones, the bones act as a series of connected levers that can then move the body or outside objects in any direction desired.

Bones provide the structural support. The muscles house the contractile units that have the ability to convert chemical energy into mechanical energy, which generates the force necessary for movement. The joints hold the

Figure 2.1 The skeleton

1. Cranium
2. Clavicle
3. Sternum
4. Rib
5. Humerus
6. Radius
7. Ulna
8. Pubis
9. Carpus
10. Metacarpals
11. Phalanges
12. Femur
13. Patella
14. Tibia
15. Fibula
16. Tarsus
17. Metatarsals
18. Phalanges

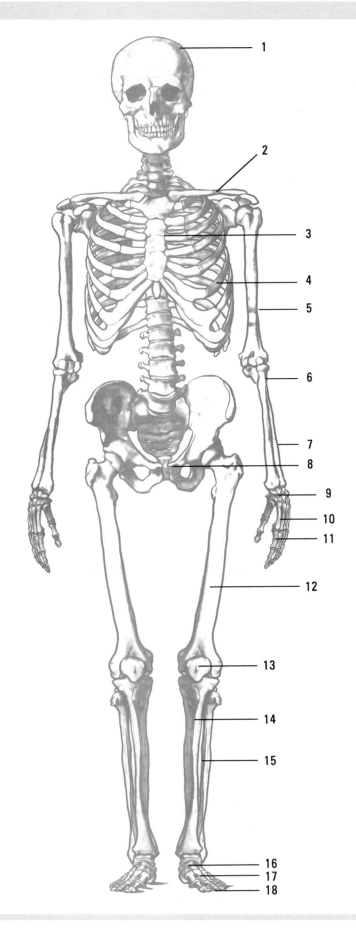

19. Cervical vertebrae (7)
20. Scapula
21. Thoracic vertebrae (12)
22. Lumbar vertebrae (5)
23. Ilium
24. Sacrum
25. Ischium

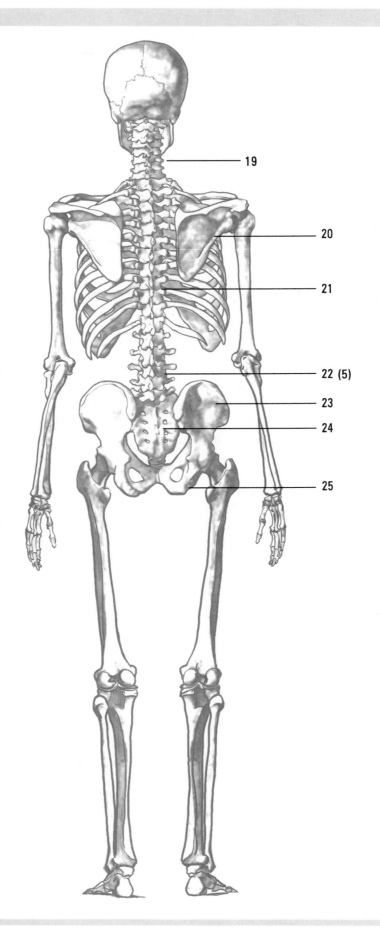

19

20

21

22 (5)

23

24

25

structure together and transmit the created internal forces through the bony levers of the body to the external environment.

All of these components are completely interdependent and cannot act separately to achieve any movement whatsoever. A muscle cannot even undergo an isometric contraction without using the bones and joints for stabilization.

We will briefly discuss each of these three components' makeup and function, individually at first and then collectively as they relate to movement. Learning how the body moves and the role each component plays to produce the movement will better enable you to understand how each exercise challenges the body. This will also help you see the reasoning behind the exercise techniques taught in this book.

The Skeleton

The human body contains approximately 206 bones. They provide a framework that supports the soft tissues so the body can maintain its form and erect posture. Some bones serve as protectors for certain vital organs. Others work together to act as a system of levers the muscles can use to move the body or external objects. Bones can produce certain blood cells and also serve as storage centers for several essential minerals. Bones may be divided or classified into two basic groups known as the axial skeleton and the appendicular skeleton.

The axial skeleton consists of 80 bones that make up the head, neck, and trunk. It houses the spine, which is the main support column for the body. Therefore, the axial skeleton's position and role during any resisted movement is always of particular concern and primary importance.

The appendicular skeleton consists of 126 bones that form the shoulders, pelvis, arms, legs, hands, and feet. Most of the movements we can perform and use for resistance training are a result of moving the bones of the appendicular skeleton.

While the appendicular skeleton moves against the resistance, the axial skeleton supports and stabilizes the body. Figure 2.1 shows a diagram of the human skeleton, including the names of all the major bones.

The Joints

A joint is the connection point between two bones. The stability and integrity of all joints are maintained by fibrous strands of connective tissue known as ligaments. These hold the bones together. Some joints allow for a great deal of movement, while others have virtually no movement capacity at all. Fibrous joints allow very little if any movement due to the small amount of space between the bone endings. The joints of the skull, the joint between the radius and ulna of the lower arm, and the joint between the distal end of the tibia and fibula of the lower leg are all fibrous. Cartilaginous joints have only a very limited capacity for movement. Examples are the joints that connect the ribs to the sternum and the intervertebral disks of the spine. Synovial joints account for most of the joints in the human body. They allow for considerable and varying amounts of movement. Joints can be categorized by their type of movement and by defining the number of directions in which they can rotate around their given axis.

Types of Joints

Uniaxial joints have only one axis of rotation and operate much like hinges. The elbow joint and the joints connecting the phalanges of the fingers are examples of uniaxial joints (figure 2.2).

Biaxial joints, such as the wrist and the ankle, allow movement in two perpendicular axes (figure 2.3).

Multiaxial joints have at least three axes of motion and can create movement in all three perpendicular planes. The shoulder and hip, which are ball-and-socket joints, are examples of multiaxial joints (figure 2.4).

The Muscles

The human body contains more than 600 muscles. We will discuss only the larger voluntary muscles known as skeletal muscle. Skeletal muscle contains contractile units that have the ability to convert chemical energy into mechanical energy, thus enabling the muscle to contract or shorten. Muscles cannot independently lengthen. They can lengthen only by contracting the opposing muscles. When one muscle (the agonist) contracts, the opposite muscle (the antagonist) lengthens.

In order for muscles to contract at all, they must be attached to the bones. Strong, fibrous tissues located at each end of the muscle, called tendons, accomplish this. The attachment of the muscle at the proximal end of the bone (the end closer to

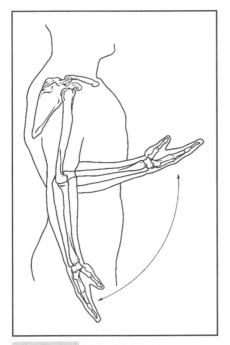

Figure 2.2 Uniaxial joint

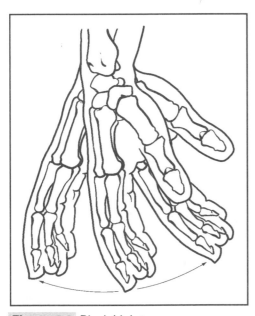

Figure 2.3 Biaxial joint

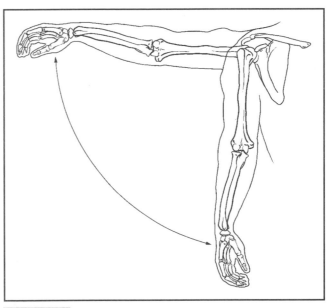

Figure 2.4 Multiaxial joint

Figure 2.5 The muscles

1. Sternocleidomastoid
2. Trapezius (upper)
3. Anterior deltoid
4. Medial deltoid
5. Clavicular pectoralis major
6. Sternal pectoralis major
7. Biceps brachii
8. Serratus anterior
9. Rectus abdominis
10. Internal oblique (underlying)
11. External oblique
12. Brachioradialis
13. Palmaris longus
14. Flexors
15. Extensors
16. Tensor fasciae latae
17. Pectineus
18. Sartorius
19. Adductor longus
20. Gracilis
21. Rectus femoris
22. Vastus lateralis
23. Vastus medialis
24. Gastrocnemius
25. Tibialis anterior
26. Peroneus longus
27. Extensors
28. Soleus

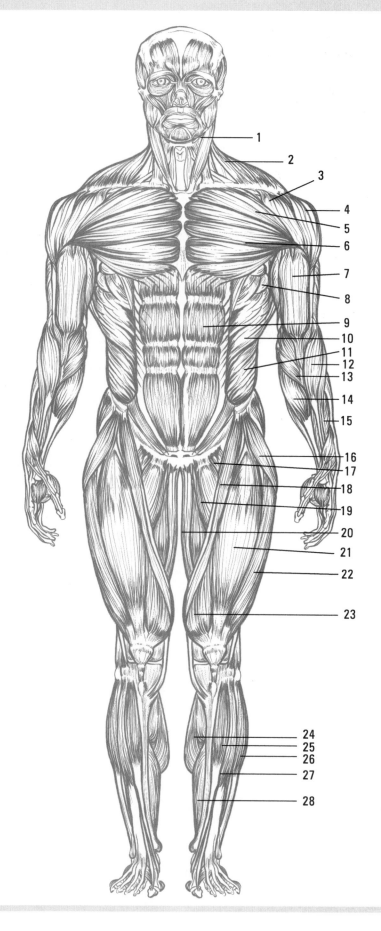

29. Levator scapulae (underlying)
30. Rhomboids (underlying)
31. Posterior deltoid
32. Trapezius (middle)
33. Teres major
34. Latissimus dorsi
35. Trapezius (lower)
36. Triceps brachii (lateral head)
37. Triceps brachii (long head)
38. Erector spinae
39. Gluteus medius
40. Gluteus maximus
41. Biceps femoris
42. Semitendinosus
43. Semimembranosus
44. Popliteus

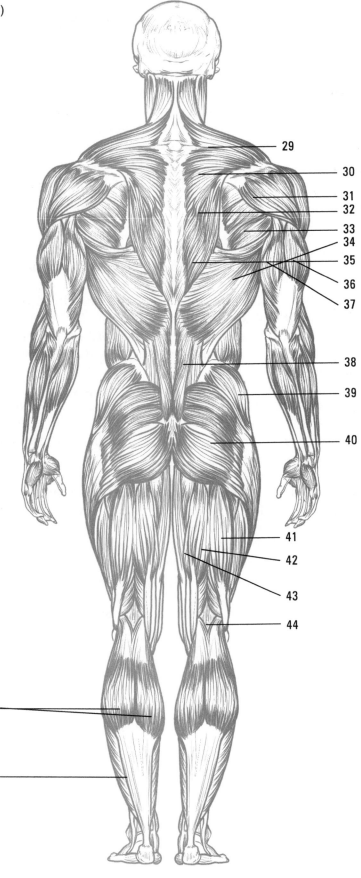

the body) is considered the muscle's origin. The attachment at the distal end of the bone (the end farther from the body) is referred to as the muscle's insertion. The origin of the trunk muscles are always at the upper or superior attachment, while the insertion is found at the lower or inferior attachment.

Muscles have different contraction capacities and therefore can play different roles depending on the desired movement. A muscle can contract concentrically while it shortens or pulls. This typically results in a movement in which the muscle acts as a primary mover.

A muscle can also contract concentrically in cooperation with other muscles. The synergistic effort results in a movement that the muscle would not have been able to perform completely on its own. In this situation, the muscle would be considered a synergist or an assistor.

On the other hand, a muscle may also contract eccentrically while it lengthens. Even though it is elongating, the muscle can still be contracting enough to help slow the movement. In this case, the muscle acts like a brake to control the body as it moves.

Yet another possibility is that a muscle could be contracting isometrically while it neither shortens nor lengthens. A muscle may utilize varying degrees of these isometric contractions in order to stabilize the body and certain joints during an exercise. The muscle would be working as a stabilizer in this situation.

A muscle may also contract to prevent an undesired effect of another contracting muscle. It would then be acting as a neutralizer. For example, the abdominal muscles neutralize part of the effects of the hip extensors and erector spinae as we walk. Neutralization prevents the spine from reaching large degrees of hyperextension.

As you learn the various movements the human body is capable of performing, the roles and responsibilities of each muscle during each joint motion will become clearer. Figure 2.5 is a diagram of all the major skeletal muscles involved in resistance training. Learn their names, placement, and the primary movements they produce as best you can. This will make you more aware of your body's internal movements during any given exercise. It will also help you focus on the proper muscles and execute the correct form. If you are a personal trainer, fitness instructor, or coach, it is extremely important that you know this information in order to more competently teach and train your clients and athletes.

CHAPTER 3

MUSCLE AND JOINT ANALYSIS

Describing movement can be difficult due to the variety of motions possible by the human body. An endless combination of movements or joint motions can be, or need to be, performed to accomplish even the simplest of activities. For example, consider how many different joint motions and muscular contractions you use simply to brush your hair or to put on a pair of pants.

To simplify and be able to discuss movement in a way that can be best understood, a consistent reference format must be used. To accomplish this, the following conventions are followed.

- Each joint motion is considered in isolation.
- Three perpendicular planes of motion are used for reference.
- All movements are described in relation to the standard anatomic position of the body.

The body is considered in its anatomic position when a person is standing upright, head facing forward, feet straight ahead, and arms hanging by the sides with palms turned forward (figure 3.1).

The three perpendicular planes of motion divide the body into different sections or halves. Each plane has two acceptable names. Due to their

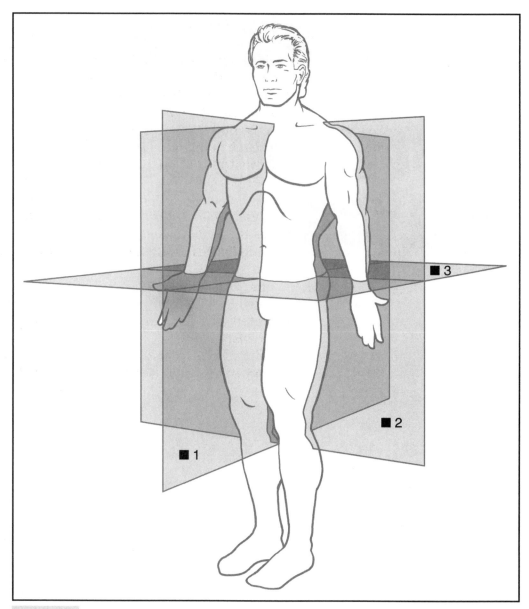

Figure 3.1 Three planes of motion

descriptive nature, I like to use the names shown in the following list. Most people remember these names more easily because they tell you exactly how to divide the body.

1. The median plane—divides the body down the middle into left and right halves

2. The frontal plane—divides the body into front and back halves

3. The horizontal plane—divides the body horizontally into upper and lower halves

Muscle Activation Analysis

In addition to the major joint motions of the human body, we are now ready to learn which muscles are used to create those motions. Knowing which muscles are responsible for producing each joint motion makes it easier to determine what exercises will best train which muscles.

We will go through the body joint by joint and list the muscles that actively contract to produce each joint motion. These muscles are known as the primary movers and assistors. Other muscles may also be working to neutralize or stabilize. However, it is the primary movers that are the targeted muscles for any given exercise. (See chapter 2, the Muscles section.)

Therefore anytime you want to develop a certain muscle, simply find an exercise that produces the joint motion where that muscle acts as a primary mover. Use the following figures as a reference for matching joint motions to the muscles.

Certain joint motions of the wrist, ankle, hands, feet, and neck are not shown in this text. Though you may wish to work these motions as well, most of them are already incorporated in other activities and exercises. They are not typically worked in a resistance-training program except for rehabilitation or after a work-related injury. If you or your client have recently experienced an injury or have a history of any injury, see a physician before beginning any exercise program.

Joint Motions of the Median Plane

The median plane (also known as the sagittal plane) divides the body down the middle into symmetrical right and left halves (figure 3.2). Any movement parallel to this plane, that is, any movement that brings a part of the body forward or backward, transpires in the median plane. The actual joint motions distinctive to the median plane are referred to as flexion and extension. Flexion is usually any motion that takes a body part forward from the anatomic position. Exceptions to this are flexion of the knee, which brings the lower leg back, and dorsiflexion of the ankle, which brings the foot up. Extension is usually any motion that brings a body part backward from its anatomic position. An exception to this is extension of the ankle, which pulls the foot down. Ankle extension is also commonly referred to as plantar flexion.

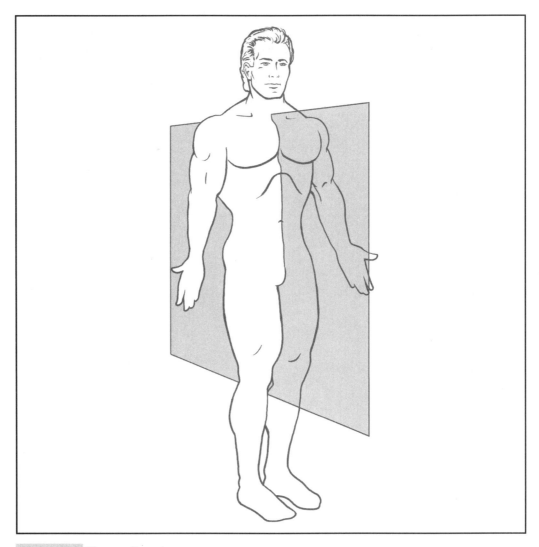

Figure 3.2 The median plane

Joint Motions of the Median Plane

ANKLE FLEXION/EXTENSION

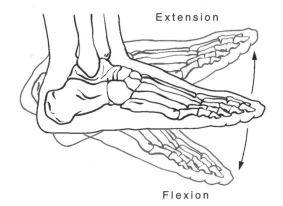

MUSCLES USED IN FLEXION

Tibialis anterior
Extensor hallucis longus
Extensor digitorum longus
Peroneus tertius

MUSCLES USED IN EXTENSION

Triceps surae (gastrocnemius and soleus)
Peroneus longus
Peroneus brevis
Flexor hallucis longus
Tibialis posterior
Flexor digitorum longus

KNEE FLEXION/EXTENSION

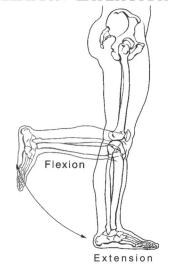

MUSCLES USED IN FLEXION

Semitendinosus
Semimembranosus
Biceps femoris
Popliteus
Gastrocnemius
Sartorius
Gracilis

MUSCLES USED IN EXTENSION

Quadriceps (rectus femoris)
Quadriceps (vastus medialis)
Quadriceps (vastus lateralis)
Quadriceps (vastus intermedius)
Tensor fasciae latae
Gluteus maximus (superficial part only)

HIP FLEXION/EXTENSION

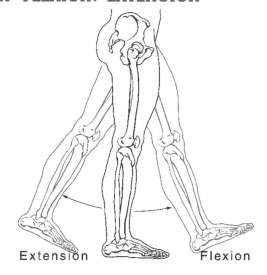

MUSCLES USED IN FLEXION

Psoas
Iliacus
Rectus femoris
Tensor fasciae latae
Gluteus minimus (anterior)
Gluteus medius (anterior)
Sartorius
Pectineus

MUSCLES USED IN EXTENSION

Gluteus maximus
Biceps femoris (long head)
Semimembranosus
Semitendinosus
Gluteus medius (posterior part)

Joint Motions of the Median Plane

TRUNK FLEXION/EXTENSION

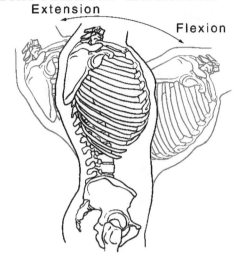

MUSCLES USED IN FLEXION

Rectus abdominis
Internal obliques
External obliques

MUSCLES USED IN EXTENSION

Erector spinae
Iliocostalis
Longissimus
Spinalis

SHOULDER FLEXION/EXTENSION

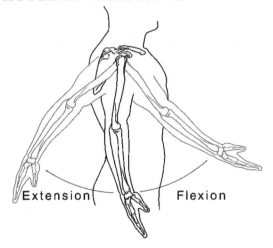

MUSCLES USED IN FLEXION

Anterior deltoid
Pectoralis major (clavicular)
Coracobrachialis

MUSCLES USED IN EXTENSION

Latissimus dorsi
Teres major
Posterior deltoid

Joint Motions of the Median Plane

ELBOW FLEXION/EXTENSION

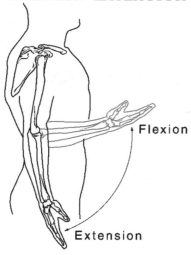

Flexion

Extension

MUSCLES USED IN FLEXION
Biceps brachii
Brachialis
Brachioradialis

MUSCLES USED IN EXTENSION
Triceps long head
Triceps lateral head
Triceps medial head
Anconeus

WRIST FLEXION/EXTENSION

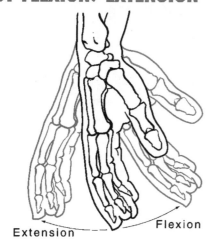

Extension   Flexion

MUSCLES USED IN FLEXION
Wrist flexors

MUSCLES USED IN EXTENSION
Wrist extensors

Joint Motions of the Frontal Plane

The frontal plane (also known as the coronal plane) divides the body into anterior, or front, and posterior, or back, halves (figure 3.10). Any movement parallel to this plane, that is, any movement that brings a part of the body in toward the median or out away from the median, transpires in the frontal plane. The actual joint motions distinctive to the frontal plane are referred to as adduction and abduction. Adduction is any motion that brings a limb or body part toward the median or centerline of the body. Abduction is any motion that brings a limb out away from the median or centerline of the body. Lateral flexion of the neck and trunk are the other joint motions that also take place in the frontal plane.

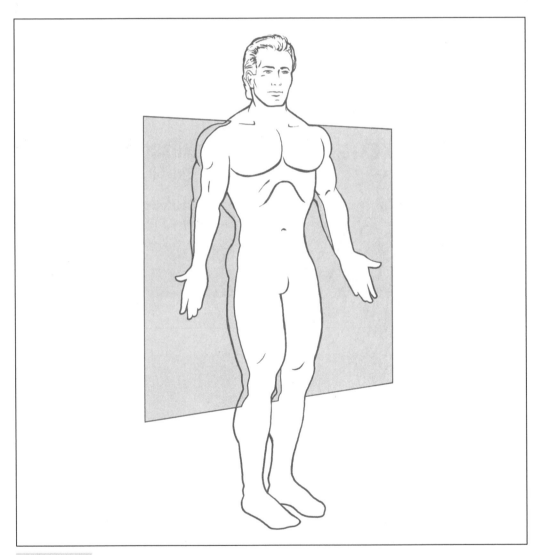

Figure 3.10 The frontal plane

Joint Motions of the Frontal Plane

ANKLE ADDUCTION\ABDUCTION (INVERSION\EVERSION)

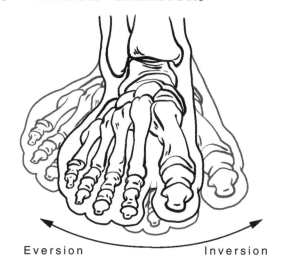

Eversion   Inversion

MUSCLES USED IN ADDUCTION

Extensor hallucis longus
Tibialis anterior
Tibialis posterior
Flexor digitorum longus
Flexor hallucis longus
Triceps surae

MUSCLES USED IN ABDUCTION

Peroneus longus, brevis
Peroneus tertius
Extensor digitorum longus (lateral part)

HIP ADDUCTION/ABDUCTION

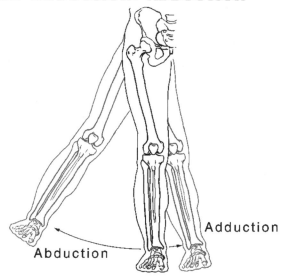

Adduction
Abduction

MUSCLES USED IN ADDUCTION

Adductor magnus
Adductor longus
Adductor brevis
Pectineus
Gracilis
Psoas
Iliacus
Biceps femoris (long head)
Gluteus maximus (deep part)

MUSCLES USED IN ABDUCTION

Gluteus medius
Gluteus minimus
Tensor fasciae latae
Gluteus maximus (superficial part)
Piriformis (accessory)
Obturators (accessory)
Gemelli (accessory)
Sartorius (accessory)

Joint Motions of the Frontal Plane

TRUNK LATERAL FLEXION

Flexion

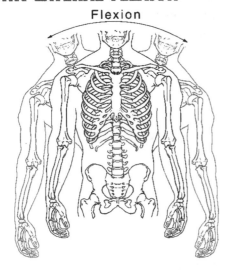

MUSCLES USED IN FLEXION

Internal oblique
Rectus abdominis
Erector spinae
Quadratus lumborum

SCAPULA ELEVATION

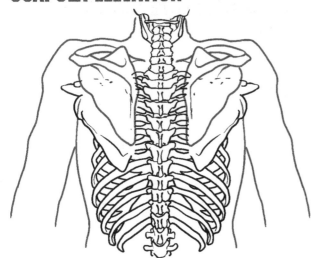

Elevation

MUSCLES USED IN ELEVATION

Levator scapulae
Trapezius (upper)
Rhomboids

Joint Motions of the Frontal Plane

SCAPULA DEPRESSION

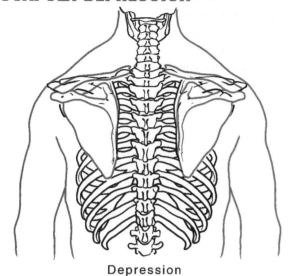

Depression

MUSCLES USED IN DEPRESSION

Trapezius (lower)
Pectoralis minor
Serratus anterior (lower)

SCAPULA PROTRACTION

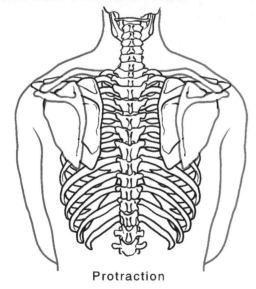

Protraction

MUSCLE USED IN PROTRACTION

Serratus anterior

Joint Motion of the Frontal Plane

SCAPULA RETRACTION

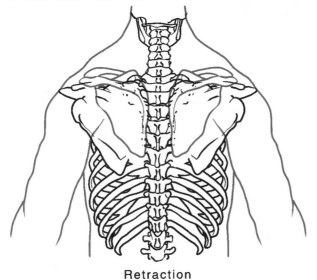

Retraction

MUSCLES USED IN RETRACTION

Rhomboids
Trapezius (middle)
Trapezius (upper)
Trapezius (lower)

SCAPULA UPWARD ROTATION

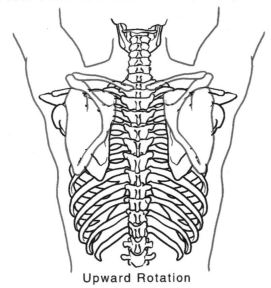

Upward Rotation

MUSCLES USED IN UPWARD ROTATION

Trapezius (upper)
Serratus anterior
Trapezius (lower)

Joint Motion of the Frontal Plane

SCAPULA DOWNWARD ROTATION

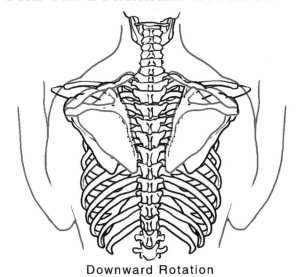

Downward Rotation

MUSCLES USED IN DOWNWARD ROTATION

Rhomboids
Levator scapulae

SHOULDER ADDUCTION/ ABDUCTION

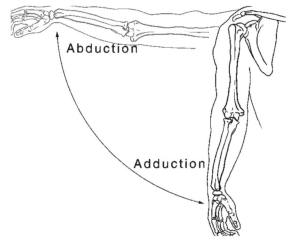

Abduction

Adduction

MUSCLES USED IN ADDUCTION

Latissimus dorsi
Pectoralis major
Teres major
Teres minor (accessory)
Coracobrachialis (accessory)
Biceps brachii short head (accessory)

MUSCLES USED IN ABDUCTION

Medial deltoid
Supraspinatus
Infraspinatus (accessory)
Biceps brachii long head (accessory)

Joint Motions of the Horizontal Plane

The horizontal plane (also known as the transverse plane) divides the body horizontally into superior, or upper, and inferior, or lower, halves (figure 3.21). Any movement parallel to this plane, that is, any movement that rotates a limb or body part in toward the body or out away from the body, transpires in the horizontal plane. The actual joint motions distinctive to the horizontal plane are median, or internal rotation, and lateral, or external rotation. Internal rotation is any motion that rotates a body part in toward the median or centerline of the body. External rotation is any movement that rotates a body part out away from the median or centerline of the body.

Both supination (which is similar to external rotation) and pronation (which is similar to internal rotation) of the forearm also occur in this plane. Horizontal adduction and abduction are also considered joint motions of the horizontal plane.

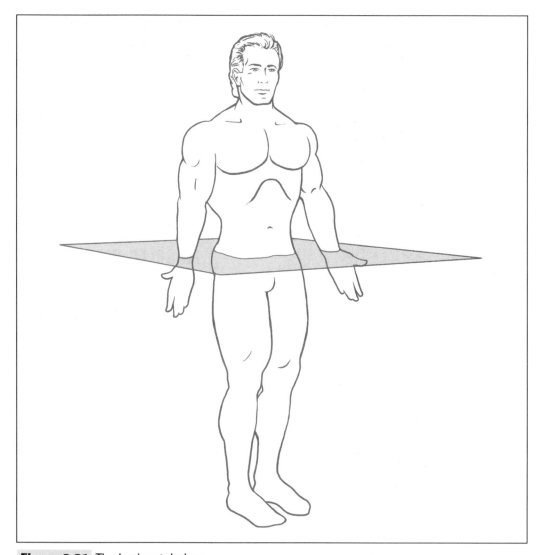

Figure 3.21 The horizontal plane

Joint Motions of the Horizontal Plane

KNEE INTERNAL/EXTERNAL ROTATION

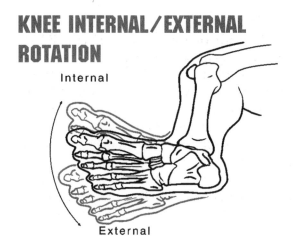

Internal

External

MUSCLES USED IN INTERNAL ROTATION

Sartorius
Semitendinosus
Gracilis
Popliteus

MUSCLES USED IN EXTERNAL ROTATION

Tensor fasciae latae
Gluteus maximus (superficial part)
Biceps femoris (long and short head)

HIP INTERNAL/EXTERNAL ROTATION

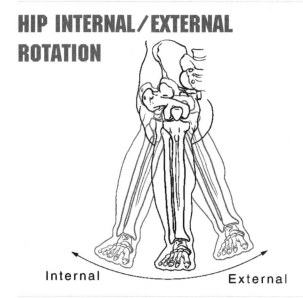

Internal   External

MUSCLES USED IN INTERNAL ROTATION

Gluteus medius
Gluteus minimus
Tensor fasciae latae

MUSCLES USED IN EXTERNAL ROTATION

Gluteus maximus
Piriformis
Obturators
Gemelli
Quadratus femoris
Biceps femoris
Adductors

TRUNK ROTATION

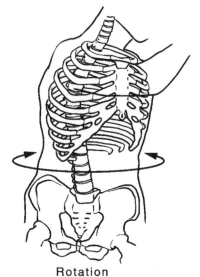

Rotation

MUSCLES USED IN ROTATION

External oblique
Rectus abdominis
Erector spinae

Joint Motions of the Horizontal Plane

SHOULDER HORIZONTAL ADDUCTION/ABDUCTION

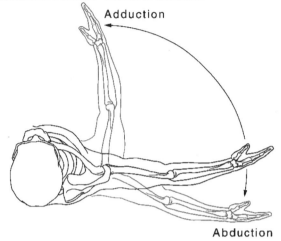

Adduction

Abduction

MUSCLES USED IN ADDUCTION

Pectoralis major (sternal)
Pectoralis major (clavicular)
Anterior deltoid
Coracobrachialis (accessory)
Biceps brachii (accessory)

MUSCLES USED IN ABDUCTION

Posterior deltoid
Trapezius (upper)
Trapezius (middle)
Rhomboids
Latissimus dorsi
Teres major (accessory)

SHOULDER INTERNAL/EXTERNAL ROTATION

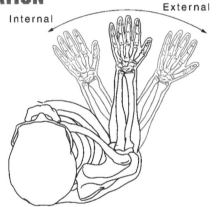

Internal

External

MUSCLES USED IN INTERNAL ROTATION

Subscapularis
Latissimus dorsi (accessory)
Teres major (accessory)
Pectoralis major (accessory)
Anterior deltoid (accessory)

MUSCLES USED IN EXTERNAL ROTATION

Infraspinatus
Teres minor
Posterior deltoid (accessory)

ELBOW SUPINATION/PRONATION

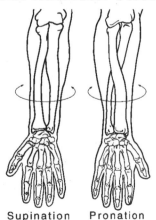

Supination   Pronation

MUSCLES USED IN SUPINATION

Biceps brachii
Supinator

MUSCLES USED IN PRONATION

Pronator teres
Pronator quadratus
Brachioradialis
Anconeus (accessory)

CHAPTER 4

EXERCISE FORM AND TECHNIQUE

Every resistance-training exercise is unique, but certain specifics pertain to all the exercises. These specifics are based on the anatomy and the biomechanical functioning of the human body. The way in which these specifics are viewed is what determines the form and technique to be used for each exercise.

These specifics are the alignment of the resistance, the positioning of the body, the motion of the exercise, the techniques used, and the progression of the exercises. We will also touch on program design and the aspects of balance, intensity, volume, duration, and the frequency of resistance training.

Alignment

The type of resistance used will make little difference and will not be effective if it is not properly aligned to the targeted muscle. Muscles tend to contract along the axis of their fibers. Therefore, alignment is matching the direction of the resistance in direct opposition to the pull of the fibers of the targeted muscles. For example, the fibers of the chest predominantly run horizontally. They originate from the sternum and clavicle and attach to the upper part of the humerus. This means the fibers will contract horizontally and pull the arms together in front of the body. Therefore, to align the resistance to the muscle properly, the resistance should oppose that motion of pulling the arms together while they are in a horizontal position. As you can see, it is extremely helpful to know how the muscles move the body in order to align them effectively with the resistance.

Aligning the Resistance to the Body

Movable types of resistance need to be placed in such a way as to provide resistance directly opposing the targeted muscle's action. Examples of movable resistance are tubing, springs, cable machines, and to some extent, free weights.

Aligning the Body to the Resistance

With most machines, resistance is already redirected to oppose the targeted muscles. It is then the lifters' responsibility to align their bodies to the resistance. This is not always as easy as it seems. More is involved in finding the best alignment than just setting the seat adjustments.

Free Weights

Although free weights allow for the freedom of movement and placement, using them is still more a matter of aligning your body to the resistance than vice versa. This reasoning is quite simple. Free weights do not directly provide the resistance—gravity does. Gravity can provide resistance in only one direction, and that direction is straight down. With this obvious limitation on direction, you must have some knowledge about how the body works in order to train all of your muscles using free weights. You must be able to align both the resistance and your body properly for free weights to be efficient and safe. This is the main reason why most of the exercises in this book utilize free weights.

Positioning

The positioning of the body during resistance training is how people bend or straighten, lift or lower, twist or turn, and hold or stabilize their bodies before and during the exercise. The main two goals we wish to accomplish by proper positioning are the same goals that this book is based on—receiving a higher level of efficiency and providing a greater degree of safety. Therefore, the definition of positioning is the way in which people move and stabilize their entire bodies before and during any resisted exercise to obtain the maximum efficiency for the targeted muscles and provide for the minimum risk due to injury.

Positioning of the Spine

Although the entire body needs to be properly positioned during resistance training, the axial skeleton and its immediate attachments are of greatest concern and require particular attention. Correctly positioning and stabilizing the spine, neck, and pelvis during resistance-training exercises are especially important. To see better how these areas should be positioned during exercise, you should first be aware of how they are positioned when held or stabilized at rest. Not everyone has the same degree of spinal curvature, and some may have spinal abnormalities as can be seen in figure 4.1. If you or someone you are training has any of these abnormalities or any type of back problems, be sure a doctor is consulted before beginning any exercise program. Figure 4.1 shows the normal spine and the abnormal conditions of lordosis, kyphosis, and scoliosis.

Different schools of thought exist regarding the spine and exercise. Some people advocate flattening the back during most any exercise in which a bench, pad, or some sort of outside support is present. The theory behind this concept is to reduce the stress on the spine, intervertebral disks, and lower-back area by bracing them against a support. Flattening the back actually requires most people to tilt the pelvis posteriorly. The spine is in its strongest position and the disks are under the least amount of compression when the spine, neck, and pelvis are all in a neutral position with the normal arches and curvatures intact. With this in mind, I prefer to do most every exercise while keeping the lumbar spine and the cervical spine in a neutral position. The only change is a slight degree of extension or straightening through the thoracic region. To do this, we simply pull the shoulder blades

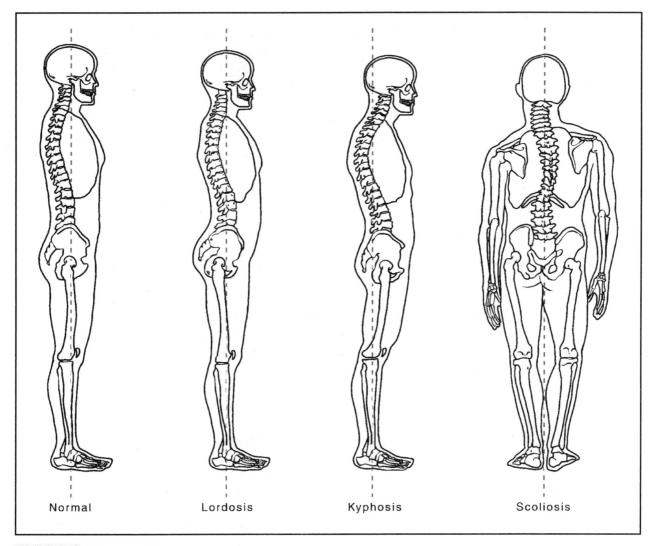

| Normal | Lordosis | Kyphosis | Scoliosis |

Figure 4.1 Spine conditions

together and lift the chest slightly up and out while maintaining the natural arch in the lumbar and cervical regions of the spine. An example of this would be soldiers standing at attention with their shoulders back and their chests out. This spinal positioning is called a ready position. Figure 4.2 shows the spine while in this position.

Positioning the spine in this manner supports weight more efficiently and still allows for the least amount of intervertebral disk compression in the cervical and lumbar regions. Instead of bracing the lower back by flattening it, you should maintain the natural arch in the lumbar spine. Maintaining this position will require stabilization from the muscles throughout the back, particularly those of the lower region. This is an added benefit. These muscles will be working to stabilize what is a natural and desirable spinal position while the targeted muscles are working against the resistance. Muscles of the trunk and lower back are typically weak links in most individuals. Using this positioning will help to strengthen and stabilize these weak links rather than pacifying them. Isn't strengthening weak muscles one of the reasons we do resistance training in the first place? (Weak links will be covered in further detail in this chapter in the section about progression.)

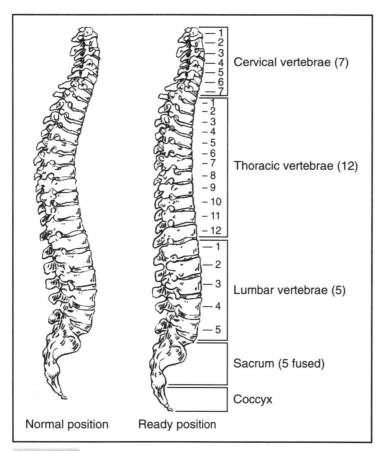

Cervical vertebrae (7)

Thoracic vertebrae (12)

Lumbar vertebrae (5)

Sacrum (5 fused)

Coccyx

Normal position   Ready position

Figure 4.2 Spine positions

Positioning During Exercise

The body is capable of many possible movements. Many of these movements and positions are easier and safer for us to achieve or hold and are considered low-risk movements or positions. Positions or movements that require a much higher level of effort to hold or achieve and have a greater chance for injury are considered high-risk movements or positions. When determining what is high risk or low risk for someone, many factors must be considered. What may be classified low risk for one individual may be a relatively high risk for someone else. A person's strength, flexibility, experience, age, and overall condition are just some of the variables that must be taken into account when attempting to decide the level of risk involved with any activity. Obviously, the involvement of the axial skeleton and pelvis are always determining factors when assessing the level of risk involved in any movement or position. Figure 4.3 shows diagrams of the spine and its possible motions.

When exercising, these motions of the spine are a primary concern and a major factor for assessing the level of risk involved. The further the exercise's

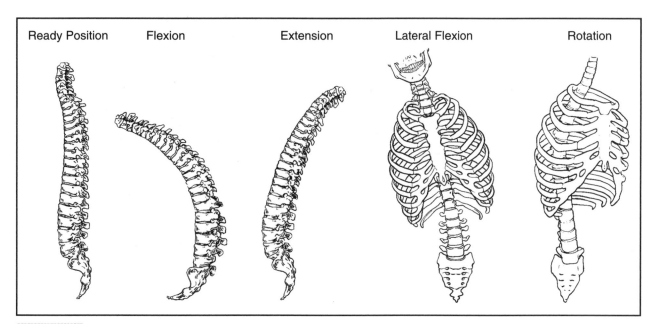

| Ready Position | Flexion | Extension | Lateral Flexion | Rotation |

Figure 4.3 Spine positions during exercise

movement takes the spine away from its natural position or out of the ready position, the higher the risk of that movement. This is especially true if a force, impact, or resistance of any type is involved.

Exercises and activities outside the gym can also become higher risk by adding other elements. For example, riding a stationary bike with a light resistance while keeping the back in proper positioning would be a relatively low-risk activity. In comparison, riding a bicycle quickly down a very bumpy hill while carrying a backpack with the spine in flexion would be a higher-risk activity.

Technique makes a great deal of difference in the level of risk involved in any activity. For example, an individual could be at less risk of injury while performing a squat with 100 pounds using good technique than while lifting a 10-pound bag of groceries out of the back of a car using poor technique. Figure 4.4 shows some examples of the ways positioning can utilize the structure and muscles of our bodies more efficiently to reduce the amount of risk involved in resistance training.

You should also be aware of the spinal positioning during stretching and other large bending motions, such as tying a shoe, and pick alternative techniques for these activities as well. (See figure 4.5.)

Thus, not all movement of the spine is bad. Movement and compressions are how the intervertebral disks receive nutrition. We are trying to discourage only the loaded movements and extreme movements.

Motion

Motion is the total movement of the body needed to perform the exercise. The motion of the exercise is based primarily on the action of the targeted muscle or muscles. Motion will vary for any given exercise according to certain limiting factors, technique, and goals of the individual.

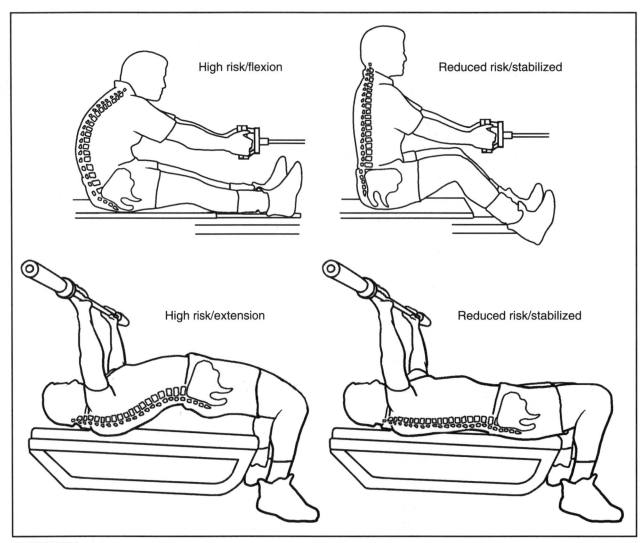

Figure 4.4 High- and low-risk activities in resistance training

Range of Motion

Range of motion typically refers to the distance in which an exercise is executed. When judging the range of motion in any given exercise, it is important to look at the movement of the body's joints and not at the bar, dumbbell, or machine. Just because the resistance or object moved a greater distance does not mean the targeted muscles contracted or stretched any farther. In many cases, it meant that some other joint and its controlling muscles were moved. This would definitely be an undesirable motion if it were not originally intended to be part of the exercise. Even if no other joint becomes involved, it is not necessary or even desirable to take the joint and the muscle to their extreme limits during resistance training. For years, exercise experts have been preaching to do exercises at a "full range of motion." After examining all of the factors related to motion, most experts feel that this is an outdated and possibly dangerous approach.

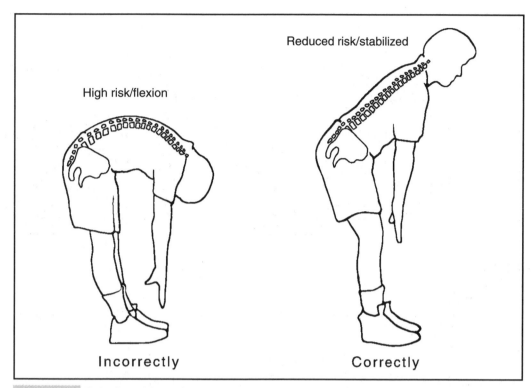

Reduced risk/stabilized

High risk/flexion

Incorrectly   Correctly

Figure 4.5 Spinal positions during stretching

Limits of Motion

The musculoskeletal system itself sets up certain anatomic and biomechanical limitations. Add to that certain physiological and neurological factors, and you should not be surprised that there is a lot of debate about how much motion should be involved in each exercise. Another strong determining factor to consider is one's goal. Here is a brief summary of the major limiting factors affecting range of motion that have been considered when designing every exercise in this book.

The Bones

Bones each have certain sizes, shapes, and protective cartilage that allow for certain movements and restrict others. During many movements, the bones may move rather easily while unresisted. However, once a formidable resistance is placed on the body, the narrow spaces between the bones become compressed and may limit their capacity for safe movement. This is particularly true for exercises involving movement of the shoulder joint.

The Joints

Since the connective tissues of the joints hold the bones in place as they are articulating or moving, the strength and stability of those joints determine a large degree of the possible range of motion. Like the bones, a joint's range of motion when moving unresisted may become reduced once the movement becomes loaded. To increase the strength and stability of the joint, you may need to increase the range of motion of the exercise. Previous injuries and the overall condition of the connective tissues, capsule, and surrounding muscles will also affect the joint's capacity for movement.

The Muscles

Muscles themselves can inhibit an exercise's range of motion in several ways. The most noticeable way is by their flexibility. If a muscle is tight, it will restrict the antagonistic movement or joint motion. The best way to overcome that is by stretching. Stretch muscles independently, without weights. Do not attempt to stretch muscles during a resisted exercise by using the weights to force the muscle to elongate. The muscles will attempt to prohibit the extreme movement and will be at a high risk for injury.

Another way in which muscles affect exercise motion is by their strength and present relationship to the joint. A degree of force angle must be present before a muscle can have much biomechanical advantage in performing any loaded joint motion. Therefore, it is important not to fully extend or lock any joint during resistance-training exercises.

Physiological processes involved in muscular contraction also affect the range of motion. A muscle's ability to contract is in direct relation to its present length. It is possible to stretch or lengthen certain muscles beyond their capacity to contract actively (via the cross-bridging within the contractile units of the muscle fibers). This is termed "active insufficiency." In such instances, the body may call upon other muscles to assist in the movement. This reduces the efficiency of the exercise for the targeted muscle and increases the risk of injury.

The Nerves

Since the body relies on nerve impulses from the brain to the muscles in order to make even the slightest movement, logically they can also affect the motion of any exercise. Part of the benefit and a large proportion of the strength increases we experience with resistance training are from developing stronger neuromuscular relationships. To put it another way, we are simply learning to use more of the muscle we already have.

As these neuromuscular relationships develop and increase, the ability to control the muscle through a certain range of motion increases. A beginning lifter or trainee usually cannot control the muscles during an exercise as efficiently, as long, or as far as someone who has been properly training for a longer period of time.

Fatigue

As you progress through a set of any exercise, you are gradually becoming more and more fatigued. The muscles and nerve impulses get weaker with each repetition. The chemicals that provide muscular energy become depleted. Therefore, if all other factors such as positioning of the body, movement speed, and resistance all remain constant, then the range of motion should decrease with the onset of fatigue. In other words, each repetition should produce slightly less movement than the preceding one until you decide to terminate the set.

The Goal

This may be a very important factor in determining what range of motion an individual will choose to use with certain exercises. Competitive athletes, for example, may have certain extreme ranges of motion required for their sport or competition. In such cases, it may be advantageous for them to train at, or closer to, those ranges of motion they will have to endure during their event. For example, a power lifter who needs to break a 90-degree angle between the upper and lower leg during the squat may need to train at these depths, at least occasionally, in order to perform that lift successfully in competition.

Be careful not to overuse or misapply this theory. For example, downhill skiers may also find themselves bouncing quickly down into those deeper ranges of motion while making a run down the slope. However, I see little benefit for these individuals to train for those brief moments by bouncing up and down into a deep squat position with a resistance. First of all, they are not going to be carrying an extra resistance while they ski. Second, why would they want to incur the similar risks in the gym that they have to endure while skiing? Most injuries to the joints are a result of cumulative damage. The more frequently you force a joint into those types of extreme ranges of motion, the more gradual damage you may suffer and the less joint integrity you may have in the long run.

Optimum Motion

So what is the bottom line on range of motion? The answer is, there isn't one. The specific range of motion is going to vary with each exercise for each person according to all of the considerations we just discussed. This will give you what we call the optimum range of motion. The optimum range of motion is the specific range that has been set for a particular exercise for a certain individual after careful consideration of the musculoskeletal and neuromuscular systems, the biomechanical factors, and the goals of the individual.

The optimum range of motion for each of the exercises in this book has been set according to all of the factors discussed in this section. The ranges of motion suggested should be suitable for most healthy individuals if the goal is to stress the primary movers maximally while protecting the joints and stabilizing the rest of the body.

Types of Motion

In chapters 2 and 3, we discussed the different joint motions that the human body is capable of performing. In this section, we will look at how those body motions translate and combine to perform different types of exercise motions.

Single-Joint Motion Exercises

These are exercises that utilize only one individual joint motion to perform the exercise. These are also referred to as isolation exercises. An example would be a tricep extension, which uses only the joint motion of elbow extension to perform the exercise.

Multiple-Joint Motion Exercises

These are exercises that require the use of two or more joint motions in order to complete the exercise. These are also commonly referred to as compound exercises. An example of this would be a leg press, which involves a hip, knee, and slight ankle extension to press the resistance.

Linear Motion Exercises

These are exercises where the path of motion follows along a straight or linear line. A chest press performed on a Smith Machine is an example of an exercise with a linear motion.

Rotational Motion Exercises

These are exercises where the path of motion is a circular rotation around a fixed axis. Many resistance training machines provide this type of motion.

Curvilinear Motion Exercises

These are exercises that include an arching motion due to the joint's natural rotation. A barbell shoulder press could be an example of an exercise with a curvilinear motion if performed with this goal.

Singular-Plane Joint Motion Exercises

These are exercises that completely transpire in a single, perpendicular plane of motion. They can be any of the above types of motions or even combinations of them as long as the total motion remains in only one plane.

Dual- or Multiple-Plane Joint Motion Exercises

These are exercises that combine two or more motions in such a manner that the motion moves through more than one plane. An example of this motion would be performing a dumbbell front deltoid press while rotating the arms and dumbbells as they are elevated.

Singular-Plane Versus Multiple-Plane Joint Motion

For most people, conducting singular-plane joint movements is preferable to multiple-plane joint movements with most resistance-training exercises. The reasoning for this goes back to the same two principles this book is based on—efficiency and safety.

Efficiency

Any time a joint begins to change direction or add a movement direction that takes the motion into a plane other than its original heading, other muscles are activated to accomplish the task. Once those muscles add their pull during the exercise, some of the resistance load is removed from the original primary movers. This results in a reduced demand on the primary movers and an increased demand on the secondary movers. This technique is fine if your goal is to stimulate as many muscles as possible with that one exercise. However, if your goal is to target a particular muscle or muscle group, staying with the original joint motion throughout the exercise would be advantageous.

Safety

If you do multiple-joint motion exercises, you must be aware of any strength differentials or weak links involved in the exercise and have the appropriate resistance set for them. Multiple-plane joint motions are natural and performed without thought for many daily activities. For example, simply brushing your hair back requires a combination of flexion, abduction, and external rotation of the shoulder joint. However, these motions are not loaded or done with a resistance. In most cases where a resistance is being used, it is best to ask the joint to perform only one motion at a time.

Technique

Each individual resistance-training exercise has its own specifics and techniques that you will learn to use to get the most benefit out of each repetition. All of the exercises in this book have their own particular set of instructions pertaining to technique. However, try to incorporate the following steps about technique into every resistance exercise you perform. By consistently practicing them, they will become second nature and enhance the efficiency and increase the safety of virtually any resistance exercise.

- **Step 1:** Before beginning, clear your mind of everything other than the exercise and determine your goal for doing this exercise. To do this, you must know the answers to the following questions:
    1. What muscle or muscles are you training, and what joint motion is produced? (The exercise needs to incorporate proper joint motion. If you are unsure, refer to the joint motion and muscle movement analysis sections in chapter 3.)
    2. Why are you doing the exercise, and what benefits do you expect? (Be sure the exercise can realistically provide the benefits you expect.)
- **Step 2:** Align the resistance to the body or the body to the resistance so that the pull of the fibers of the targeted muscles directly opposes the push or pull of the resistance.
- **Step 3:** Position the body so that it has the best possible position for support, safest angles for all joints, and the greatest ability to stabilize. Pay particular attention to the spine.
- **Step 4:** Determine the optimum range of motion for this exercise that will enable you to best train the targeted muscles and keep your proper positioning.
- **Step 5:** Stabilize. Hold your positioning, and allow no other parts of the body to move other than the ones necessary to perform the exercise. Always try to stabilize with the muscles as much as possible rather than relying on outside supports or on the skeletal system. (For example, keep a slight bend in the knees and some degree of flexion in the hips as opposed to standing straight up with the knees locked during any standing exercise.)
- **Step 6:** Focus on contracting the muscle or muscles you are targeting (the primary movers). Feel them shortening as they contract.

Visualize them pulling the bones that are moving. Try to focus on each phase:

1. Contract slowly—concentric phase.

2. Hold at the peak contraction—isometric phase.

3. Release slowly—eccentric phase.

Continue this process being sure to keep constant tension on the muscles throughout the exercise. Repetition speed should be approximately seven seconds.

■ **Step 7:** Breathe. Breathing should be purposeful, yet smooth, and rhythmic to the contraction of the muscles. With most exercises, it is best to breathe out during the concentric phase and breathe in during the eccentric phase.

Going through this step-by-step procedure each time is an important and key aspect for deriving the maximum benefit out of each rep of every set for every exercise you perform in your fitness program. At first, it may appear to be a lot of extra effort. However, once practiced, it soon becomes a habit and takes no more time to perform than would running through an exercise by just going through the motions. Once you realize your goal for the exercise and know the alignment, positioning, motion, and rhythm of breathing involved, it takes only a matter of seconds to coordinate it all together.

Progression

Most fitness professionals generally agree that anyone beginning a fitness program needs to have a starting point. Everyone needs to develop a foundation or a base on which to build the rest of a solid resistance-training program. Therefore, a base program should be designed to address the individual's needs as opposed to pursuing his or her goals.

A good foundation or base for fitness is developed by strengthening and stabilizing those areas that give us greatest support along with any areas that are at the highest risk of injury. These are considered weak links of the body. The first priority should be to strengthen and stabilize the muscles of the axial skeleton, pelvis, knees, shoulder, and scapular joints of the body along with any other individual weak links present. This needs to be accomplished prior to proceeding toward training for any personal goals.

For example, a person's goal may be to increase overall upper-body muscle mass particularly in the chest and back regions. This means that, eventually, a fair amount of chest and back exercises will be included in this individual's program. However, during his or her base building stage, it is far more important to strengthen and stabilize the rotator cuff, shoulder, and scapular muscles prior to progressing to a lot of chest or back exercises.

A weak link can be defined as any muscle, joint, or even bone that limits the rest of the body's ability to perform to its full capacity during a certain exercise or activity. Weak links can be naturally occurring, as a result of an injury, or as an inherent factor involved in a particular exercise or activity.

Naturally occurring weak links for many people are the low back, neck, knee joints, and shoulder joints. Ankles, elbows, and wrists can also be weak points for some people. With this in mind, a beginning program would concentrate on stabilizing these areas by strengthening the following muscle groups:

- The muscles of the trunk and lower back. This means all of the abdominal, spinal, low-back, and pelvic muscles.
- The muscles of the neck. This usually does not require much more resistance than simply stabilizing or slightly moving the weight of the head at different angles.
- The rotator cuff muscles of the shoulder joint and the muscles controlling the shoulder girdle.
- The muscles operating the knee joint, particularly the quadriceps and hamstrings.
- Muscles, tendons, and ligaments controlling the ankles and wrists.

Previous injuries such as muscle, tendon, and ligament tears or bone fractures may be other weak links that need to be considered before proceeding. As always, if in doubt, see a physician before attempting any exercise.

A muscle does not have to be particularly weak to become a weak link during certain exercises. It may just be weak in comparison with other muscles involved in that exercise. For example, typically, the lower back will be the weak link in a squat no matter how strong or stable the lower back becomes. This occurs because the leg muscles responsible for actually moving the resistance are bigger and stronger than the lower-back muscles. So in this particular exercise, the legs are limited to what they can move by the amount of resistance that the lower back can support and stabilize. Therefore, the lower back could be considered the weak link during this exercise. If someone desires to work the legs with less challenge for the lower back, that individual may choose to perform a seated leg press rather than a squat. However, this could also be viewed as less benefit for the lower back.

Progression of Exercises

Numerous approaches and several factors must be considered in order to determine which exercises should proceed or follow one another. These decisions will be made differently by every trainer, instructor, and coach for each client, athlete, or individual they train. After a strong base has been developed, the selection of exercises will be determined more by an individual's goals and less by that person's initial needs.

All of the exercises in this book accurately depict the muscles you will be training and will give a description that will help provide some idea of where the exercise might be placed in a logical progression. If you have little or no experience with resistance training and are not working with a qualified trainer, I suggest beginning with machine exercises due to their safety as opposed to using free weights for most muscle groups. If, however, you are working with a qualified trainer, then using free weights may be best to learn how to move and control your body without the constriction of a machine. Some exercises, such as trunk exercises and squats, may not require any resistance other than your body weight at the beginning. In any case, remember that how the exercises are performed is usually far more important than which ones are selected. Begin by following the base program described in this chapter, and be sure to follow closely the step-by-step instructions provided in this book for these exercises and any others you may choose.

Progression Within Exercises

Progression within exercises can be accomplished in ways that are less obvious than increasing the weight, repetitions, or sets. An exercise can progress when you develop the ability to demonstrate greater control, improve technique, establish a greater range of optimum motion, or better stabilize your positioning. Any of these changes can be progressive and work the muscles more efficiently.

Positioning is one of the most visible yet most often overlooked ways to achieve progression within an exercise. By placing the body in different positions relative to gravity, the machine, or the resistance, you can challenge the body in different manners. For example, doing virtually any exercise while standing will work more overall muscles than doing the same exercise from a seated position. By standing in the proper position, you will raise your center of gravity and work the muscles of the legs, hips, and back to a higher degree than when you are sitting. (You will also remove a large amount of compression from the intervertebral disks of the spine, particularly in the region of the lower back, when you move from a seated to standing position.)

However, many people may not be able to perform the exercise efficiently from a standing position at first. As previously stated, the spine and lower-back areas are typically weak links for many people. These areas may require some individual strengthening through other exercises prior to attempting exercises in a standing position. Figure 4.6 shows a logical progression that can be used for exercises like a dumbbell biceps flexion.

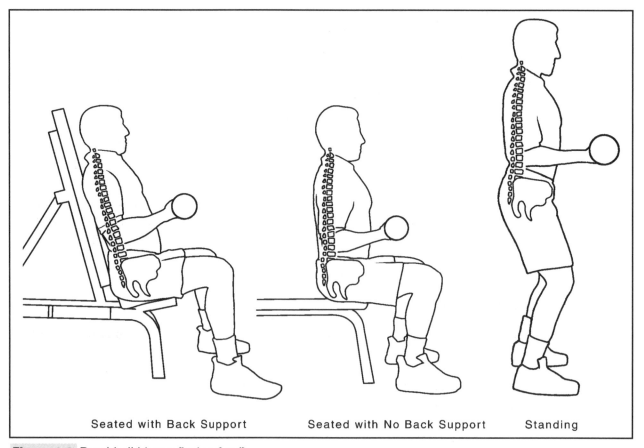

Seated with Back Support   Seated with No Back Support   Standing

Figure 4.6 Dumbbell biceps flexion (curl)

Each step in this progression demands more from the muscles that stabilize the pelvis, spine, and scapula. When viewed with a wholistic approach, each step becomes a more challenging and a more beneficial exercise even though the weight may stay the same. You may have to begin performing this particular exercise with only one arm at a time. This would require the back to stabilize only half the amount of weight as it would when using both arms. You may also simply use a lighter weight load.

Adjusting the angle of the body prior to performing a trunk flexion is another example of how positioning can be used to progress within an exercise. To begin with, I would suggest starting at an incline position. In this position, gravity would assist flexing the trunk, making it easier to accomplish a full contraction of the abdominals. Once this stage has been mastered, progress to a flat position where gravity is more neutral. The next step would be to progress to a declined position where gravity would be resisting the abdominal muscles as they flex the trunk at an upward angle.

A similar positioning sequence could be used to achieve a progression for push-ups. Begin with an inclined position by placing your hands against a wall, desk, or on a bench depending on the level of resistance desired. Once this is mastered, then progress to a flat position by placing your hands directly onto the ground.

You may also try any of these positions resting on only one foot as opposed to both. This three-point position is more difficult to balance and stabilize than when both feet are planted, making the exercise more challenging.

These are just a few ways in which positioning can be utilized to accomplish progression. Here are some other methods you should incorporate in order to experience progress within an exercise:

- Improve your control and speed of motion.

- Attempt to perfect your form and technique with each repetition.

- Increase your ability to keep tension in the targeted muscles while consistently controlling your optimum range of motion.

- Experience a greater feel of the exercise, the associated joint motions, and the muscle response to a much deeper degree than when you first began.

The ability to make any of these changes proves that progress is being achieved within an exercise long before any additional resistance is required. Don't be in a hurry to add weight or repetitions to an exercise until you are sure you have totally mastered it.

Program Design

Program design is a subject in itself. Another book could easily be needed to cover all of the different aspects involved and all of the variables that must be considered in order to design an individual's program. This section will first provide basic information pertaining to the variables of program design. Second, it will provide a few sample resistance-training routines beginning with a base program and then progressing to more challenging routines.

You need to realize that fitness is not a result of a program, it is the result of a process. Each exercise routine should be viewed as only a step in the process.

As your body adapts to each program, certain results and benefits are achieved. In order to progress and continue to receive the desired results, your body must continue to be challenged by adapting to new and more challenging programs. When designing a new exercise program, you should consider and plan for variables such as intensity, volume, duration, frequency, recovery, and balance.

Intensity

This refers to the amount of stress provided by an exercise, typically the amount of resistance being used. I recommend that you increase the resistance the least amount possible after you can complete your repetition goal with relative ease and with nearly perfect form. For cardiovascular exercise, we may describe intensity as low, moderate, or high. For resistance training, we describe intensity as light, challenging, and failure. Failure refers to *momentary muscular failure*. This is described as the point at which the muscle can no longer generate enough force to complete another repetition at the desired optimum range of motion while maintaining proper alignment and positioning.

Volume

This refers to the length of time the exercise is engaged. In resistance-training exercises, this typically means the number of repetitions and sets done per exercise. The recommendation for someone interested in general fitness is one to three sets consisting of about eight to 12 repetitions of each exercise. During a base program, I suggest only one to two sets with 12-17 repetitions for most exercises.

Duration

This refers to the length of time the training session requires. Typical resistance-training routines usually require 30 to 60 minutes. However, even 15-minute sessions can be of great benefit for most people if performed often enough.

Frequency

This refers to how often the training sessions are done. Experts generally recommend that each muscle should be trained approximately two to three times a week. This can be accomplished with a whole-body routine done the recommended two to three times a week or by alternating split routines performed several times a week. The more times a week you train, the more you can split your routines and muscle groups apart. Your goals and your available time for training are the main factors that will determine the type of routine you choose and the frequency of your workouts.

Frequency can also be affected by other factors such as your ability to recover and your overall condition. Listening to your body and altering the frequency of your workouts as needed is important.

Recovery

This refers to the amount of rest necessary for the muscles to recover and begin to adapt to the stress applied during training. Dependent on the training goal, a typical rest period between sets for the same muscle group is somewhere between 30 to 90 seconds but may range up to five minutes or more for certain types of training. This is not to say that you must rest the entire body. You may choose to perform two or more exercises back to back with little or no rest between them. These are called *supersets* and should combine exercises for different or opposing muscle groups.

Recovery between training sessions will depend on how often you train and the type of training program. Experts recommend allowing at least 48 hours before training any muscle again. Larger muscles typically take longer to recover than smaller ones, so larger ones may need more time between sessions. More intense training, greater volume, or longer session duration will also demand longer recovery periods. Watch for symptoms of overtraining such as persistent muscle soreness, aching joints, fatigue, or an increase in resting heart rate. Any of these symptoms may be signals that you are not allowing enough time to recover properly.

Balance

An individual's fitness program should be balanced. This means that the end result should provide a proper ratio of work for all muscle groups. This does not mean that the program itself always has to be balanced perfectly. The human body is created with natural muscular imbalances. Certain muscles are designed to be larger and stronger than others. Larger muscle groups may therefore require more sets, repetitions, or resistance to challenge them than the smaller muscles. A person may have certain muscles that they need or desire to work more than others. Some people may participate in activities that challenge and develop certain muscles yet completely neglect others. A balanced program would be one that considers the innate engineering of the human body and is designed to respect or compensate for all muscular imbalances.

Exercise Selection

Once your goals and needs have been assessed and all the program variables of intensity, volume, duration, frequency, recovery, and balance have been determined, the only thing remaining is to select the exercises. Exercise selection begins by choosing those exercises that best meet the needs of the individual and then developing a base as previously described.

The following scenario is set for the average person who has not been involved in resistance training for at least six months. It makes no real difference whether the person is male or female as long as the goal is general fitness and that person desires to increase strength, develop muscle tone, and reduce body fat. Since intensity levels are determined by each individual's present strength and fitness level, any person from 15 to 65 years of age may be able to begin with this base program. We will assume that you plan to engage in resistance training two to three times a week and are free from any health risks and injuries. It is always a good idea to consult your physician before beginning an exercise program.

Working with a professional trainer, at least in the beginning, may also be beneficial by ensuring you get a proper start. Be sure to check if the trainer is already familiar with all the alignment, positioning, optimum motion, and techniques for each exercise as presented in this book. This information is relatively new, and many changes have been made from the traditional ways in which these exercises have been taught. Quite possibly, your trainer may have not yet been exposed to this information or have had the opportunity to learn about these changes. Even so, a good trainer should be able to understand and interpret this information quickly in order to help you properly perform each exercise safely and efficiently.

Base Program—Stage I

This base program is designed to begin developing structural integrity. The selected exercises focus on strengthening and stabilizing the spine, pelvis, rotator cuff, and shoulder girdle. The volume, duration, and intensity are meant to challenge but not be so difficult as to create momentary muscular failure. (See p. 48 on Intensity.) Perform all exercises according to the descriptions and step-by-step instructions provided in the exercise sections of this book. It is important to pay close attention to the alignment, positioning, and motion. Follow the seven steps of technique (p. 43-44), with a repetition speed of about seven seconds for each exercise.

Description

Start with a 10-minute warm-up. I suggest a recumbent stationary bike due to the fact that it is easier to maintain good posture with proper spinal alignment. (See figure 4.2.) If this type of bike is not available, try walking on a treadmill or another flat surface. The focus should be on proper positioning rather than speed or time. Remember, all movement performed on earth is resisted movement so positioning is always of primary importance. The next exercise is a Body Weight Squat. Done properly, this exercise helps to develop spinal and pelvic stability while strengthening the low back, gluteals, and legs. This also closely resembles the functional daily activities of sitting and standing that we perform every day. When you have mastered these exercises, add on a Leg Press of some type to further challenge the legs but not yet load the spine. Since both of these exercises involve loaded knee flexion, I suggest also adding a Hamstring Flex to balance out the knee joint. The seated version may be best at this point because you will be stabilizing the body with proper positioning while strengthening the hamstrings. This may help to develop better posture habits while sitting throughout the day. Likewise, a Standing Hip Abduction will help with pelvic stabilization. Start by balancing on one leg while contracting the other. Progress to a multi-hip machine or a cable machine with ankle straps if available.

The next exercise is a modified Leg Raise. Be sure to begin by lifting only one leg as described for that exercise. This will strengthen the abdominal muscles as stabilizers, which is their primary role for most activities. The next exercise is the Machine or Cable Lat Row. This could possibly be the most important upper body exercise you will perform. Lat Rows stabilize and strengthen the lower and upper back and develop the scapula retractors and posterior deltoid muscles. Basically it works all the upper body muscles that are critical for proper posture. A Chest Press can be added next providing you are able to keep proper posture and positioning. Many times a certain amount of back work (i.e.

Table 4.1 Base Program–Stage I

Frequency: 2-3 days per week
Duration: 60 minutes (30 cardiovascular/warm-up, 30 resistance training/stretching)
Recovery: 60-90 seconds between sets
48-72 hours between workouts

Exercise	Volume (Sets-Repetitions)	Duration	Intensity
Warm-up stationary bike	•	10 min	low to moderate
Body weight squats	2 × 12–17 reps	•	challenging
Leg press	2 × 12–17 reps	•	challenging
Seated hamstring flex	2 × 12–17 reps	•	challenging
Machine standing hip abduction	2 × 12–17 reps	•	challenging
Leg raise	2 × 12–17 reps	•	challenging
Machine or cable seated lat row	2 × 12–17 reps	•	challenging
Machine or dumbbell chest press	2 × 12–17 reps	•	challenging
Dumbbell side delt abduction	2 × 12–17 reps	•	light
Tubing or cable shoulder internal rotation	1 × 12–17 reps	•	challenging
Dumbbell shoulder external rotation	1 × 12–17 reps	•	challenging
Quadriplex	2 × 12–17 reps	•	challenging
Inclined trunk flex	2 × 12–17 reps	•	challenging
Cardiovascular stationary bike	•	10 min	challenging
Stretching	•	5–10 min	light

Lat Rows) needs to be performed before a person is able to have the strength and ability to keep proper positioning during chest exercises. Next is a Dumbbell Side Delt Abduction. This is to help with shoulder stabilization only and should always be performed with light weight loads. (There are other, more safe, exercises that you can use to build bigger deltoids when and if that goal arises.) Cable Shoulder Internal Rotation and Dumbbell Shoulder External Rotation are next. (Be sure to do these after all your other upper body exercises.) A Quadriplex and an Incline Trunk Flex are now done to further stabilize and strengthen the trunk. Finish with 10 minutes of cardiovascular work by returning to the recumbent bike or walking. After that, perform some light stretching and cool down, and you're done!

Whole Body Routine—Stage II

After approximately four to six weeks of consistently performing the base program two to three times a week, you should now be ready to move to the next step in the fitness process. The Stage II Whole Body Routine continues to work on structural integrity, yet incorporates more joint motions and directly addresses more muscle groups.

Certain variables have also been altered in order to further challenge your body. For some exercises, the repetitions have increased, while in others, they have decreased with an expected increase in resistance. Supersets have also been added. (See p. 49.) The resistance should be set to produce the desired intensity level, from challenging all the way to momentary muscular failure. Be certain that as the intensity of your workouts increases, your form and technique also improve. No program will be of much value if its exercises are not performed safely and efficiently.

Adults 50 or more years of age may wish to keep their intensity at a challenging level, rather than progressing to the point of muscular failure. Be aware of any exercises that may increase blood pressure such as those in flat and declined positions, or exercises with overhead motion. I would suggest that people in this group halt their progression any further in this program until receiving assistance from a professional trainer.

Description

The Stage II Whole Body Routine starts off very similar to the base program. Begin with the same warm-up; you may increase the intensity and cut back a little on the duration if you need to save time for the resistance training and cardiovascular portions of this program. (If you have the time, I suggest you stay with the full 10 minutes of warm-up.) Begin again with the Body Weight Squats. Add repetitions and perform them with a slower, more controlled speed—approximately 10-12 seconds. Superset the Leg Press with the Hamstring Flex and try switching to the prone version. Notice also the increase in intensity to momentary failure for both of these exercises.

Next, add a set of Machine Standing Hip Adduction to the Machine Standing Hip Abduction in a superset fashion for increased pelvic stability. The next exercise is a Standing Hip Extension. This exercise not only strengthens the gluteus and hamstrings, it also increases lower back strength. Begin by using very light or no weight as described in the exercise section. A Machine Standing Calf Extension is added next. This is more for teaching the spine to except load than for strengthening the calves. Increased sets and intensity were added for the chest and back areas. A Cable Standing Rear Delt Row was also implemented for more deltoid work and for shoulder joint balance. Added intensity of the trunk muscles is accomplished by performing them in a

Table 4.2 Whole Body–Stage II

Frequency: 2-3 days per week
Duration: 60-90 minutes (20 cardiovascular/warm-up, 40 resistance training/stretching)
Recovery: 60-90 seconds between sets or active recovery (supersets)
48-72 hours between training sessions

Exercise	Volume (Sets-Repetitions)	Duration	Intensity
Warm-up stationary bike	•	5–10 min	low to moderate
Body weight squats	2 × 17–21 reps	•	challenging
SUPERSETS			
Leg press	2 × 12–17 reps	•	failure
Prone hamstring flex	2 × 8–12 reps	•	failure
Machine standing hip abduction	2 × 12–17 reps	•	challenging
Machine standing hip adduction	1 × 12–17 reps	•	challenging
Barbell standing hip extension	2 × 12–17 reps	•	light
Machine standing calf extension	2 × 12–17 reps	•	challenging
Machine or dumbbell chest press	1 × 12–17 reps 2 × 8–12 reps	•	challenging failure
Machine or cable seated lat row	1 × 12–17 reps 2 × 8–12 reps	•	challenging failure
Dumbbell side delt abduction	2 × 12–17 reps	•	challenging
Tubing or cable standing rear delt row	2 × 12–17 reps	•	challenging
Dumbbell shoulder external rotation	1 × 12–17 reps	•	challenging
Quadriplex	2 × 12–17 reps	•	challenging
Leg raise	2 × 12–17 reps	•	challenging
Resista-Ball trunk flex	2 × 12–17 reps	•	challenging
Cardiovascular stationary bike	•	15–30 min	challenging
Stretching	•	5–10 min	light

superset fashion and by incorporating the Resista-Ball Trunk Flex. (The Resista-Ball calls for greater stability of the trunk muscles.) You should now be capable of gradually increasing the duration and intensity of your cardiovascular work as well.

Whole Body Routine—Stage III

After approximately four to six weeks of consistently performing the Stage II Whole Body program two to three times a week, you should now be ready to progress to the next stage. You should feel gains in your strength and be aware of improvement in your overall fitness level. Slight increases in muscle tone and decreases in body fat should also start to become more noticeable. Now you can begin to focus a little more on your individual goals and a little less on your body's needs.

This routine still continues to develop good structural integrity while beginning to incorporate more advanced positioning, overhead motions, loaded spine exercises, and overall increased intensity from Stage II. More exercises are done in a similar amount of time, so they require less rest time and more supersets. You are expected to perform exercises with greater weight loads and train more often to muscular failure while still improving your form and technique.

This may be a good time to re-evaluate your goals and see if you can dedicate any more time to your overall health. Try to find time to increase your cardiovascular activities. Implement more lifestyle changes such as nightly walks, weekend activities, and dietary changes. A stronger, leaner, healthier, and more functional body is not accomplished by resistance training alone.

Description

This program begins with the same warm-up of about five to ten minutes depending on your prerogative and time schedule. You will then go to a Reverse Lunge or a Traveling Lunge. These types of lower-body exercises place your legs in asymmetrical positions and have been added to further challenge your pelvic stability, control, and overall balance. Very little, if any, added resistance is needed to accomplish this, so always keep the weight loads light. There are better exercises for actually building the gluteus and legs if that is your goal. Next are the Barbell Squats. Start light and try to perform them with the identical form that you used for the Body Weight Squats over the last two months or so. These are superset with a Machine Standing Calf Extension. Stretch and allow for some time before returning to the squats, since the back has not had a chance to really recover. A Machine Quad Extension has also been added to further develop the anterior thigh muscles. Use light weight on this and position yourself in such a manner that the hamstrings will be stretching and providing added resistance as the quadriceps contract. Increase intensity and resistance for the Standing Hip Extension and superset with a Leg Raise using both legs and with no arm support if possible. Add intensity and resistance if possible on the Dumbbell Chest Press and superset with a Cable Standing Lat Row. The standing position will now challenge the hip and legs, as well as the entire back. Overhead angles are now added with the Barbell Incline Chest Press and the Cable Lat Pulldown. Not only does this

Table 4.3 Whole Body–Stage III

Frequency:	2-3 days per week
Duration:	90 minutes (30 cardiovascular/warm-up, 60 resistance training/stretching)
Recovery:	60-90 seconds between sets or active recovery (supersets)
	48-72 hours between training sessions

Exercise	Volume (Sets-Repetitions)	Duration	Intensity
Warm-up stationary bike	•	5 min	low to moderate
Reverse or traveling lunges	2 × 12–17 reps	•	challenging
SUPERSETS			
Barbell squat	3 × 12–17 reps	•	challenging
Machine calf extension	3 × 17–21 reps	•	failure
Quad extension	2 × 12–17 reps	•	failure
Prone hamstring flex	3 × 8–12 reps	•	failure
Standing hip extension	2 × 12–17 reps	•	challenging
Declined trunk raise or leg raise	2 × 12–17 reps	•	challenging
Dumbbell chest press	1 × 12–17 reps / 2 × 8–12 reps	• / •	challenging / failure
Cable standing lat row	1 × 12–17 reps / 2 × 8–12 reps	• / •	challenging / failure
Barbell incline chest press	2 × 8–12 reps	•	failure
Cable lat pull down	2 × 8–12 reps	•	failure
Cable standing rear delt row	2 × 8–12 reps	•	failure
Cable overhead lat row	2 × 8–12 reps	•	failure
Dumbbell biceps flex	2 × 12–17 reps	•	failure
Dumbbell triceps extension	2 × 12–17 reps	•	failure
Resista-Ball trunk flex/ push-ups	2 × 12–17 reps	•	failure
Dumbbell shoulder external rotation	2 × 12–17 reps	•	challenging
Bike or treadmill	•	30–45 min	light
Stretching	•	5–10 min	light

provide additional training for the chest and back, the shoulder and scapula muscle groups are also further challenged. An Overhead Lat Row is now added and combined with the Cable Rear Delt Row for even more work for those postural muscles. A Dumbbell Biceps Flex and a Dumbbell Triceps Extension are next to finish off and help shape the arms. Then try supersetting some Push-ups, or a modified version, with the Resista-Ball Trunk Flex. Push-ups challenge the abdominals and hip flexors for pelvic and trunk stability, as well as work the upper-body muscles. Finish with some light rotator cuff work and then try to increase your cardiovascular work to 30-45 minutes if possible. If the time to finish this program is running short, perhaps try moving some of the cardiovascular training to your off days.

Program Alternatives

At times when you are attempting to follow this progression of routines, you may feel that you are not being challenged enough. On the other hand, you may feel that you are not recovering fast enough and perhaps are overtraining. Another possibility is that you do not feel that these examples are addressing your personal goals as much as you would like. This section will give you some suggestions on how to alter the routine to adjust for these individual differences.

If the routine you are on feels too easy, my first advice is to have patience. Remember, each routine is only one step in the process. These routines are designed to work first on needs, such as developing structural integrity, and second on accomplishing your goals. Next, try to focus more on your form and technique. Concentrate on performing every rep to the best of your ability. Then, if you are sure you are ready for more, you may wish to progress to the next routine a little sooner than the recommended four to six weeks. If you are already at stage three and still feel you need more, you can try adding a few sets or increase the intensity if you like. However, a better idea may be to look at increasing the frequency by adding another day or two to your program and switch to a split routine. Split routines enable you to perform more overall training by only training certain muscles each day, while letting other muscles recover. An example would be to train the lower body one day and the upper body the next. I would suggest a day off before returning again to the lower body.

If at any time you feel that the routine you are presently on is more than you are able to handle, my first suggestion would be to stop. Take a couple of extra days off and let your body recover. Then when you feel that you can proceed, reduce the volume and intensity. Cut down the number of sets for each exercise, and reduce the resistance.

Be careful when altering your own routines unless you are a fitness professional. You can easily develop muscular imbalances by overemphasizing areas you feel are important. This is especially true if you are not working opposing and supporting muscle groups within the proper ratios. Understanding the delicate balance and relationship that the muscles of the human body have with one another is a true science in itself. Therefore, a well-balanced exercise program trains the body with respect to the natural muscular imbalances we are designed to have.

Once you have mastered stage three, you should probably consult again with a fitness professional before making any major changes to your routine.

The next step toward achieving your overall goals may require an increase in frequency of four to five days a week. You would then shift from whole-body workouts to some sort of split routine as previously mentioned. This would be especially true if your goal involved larger increases in strength, power, or muscle mass.

If fat loss is your primary goal, you may wish to add a few more days of cardiovascular exercise and stick with the whole-body routines. However, it has been my experience that four- to five-day split routines can work great for these people as well if the routines are designed properly. Do not feel that only those who want huge muscles should train this often.

Whatever the goal, a good trainer should be able to direct you toward that path using various combinations of exercises in this book. By this point, you will have developed a strong base, gained strength, increased muscle tone, reduced body fat, and conditioned your body to a level that will be able to handle most anything a trainer throws at you. Good luck and good training!

CHAPTER 5

TRUNK EXERCISES

The following exercises are designed to target the different muscles of the trunk. These exercises are not presented in any special sequence such as order of importance or suggested progression. They are presented in the following order for layout design and organizational reasons only.

Abdominal exercises

Abdominal oblique exercises

Abdominal stabilization exercises

Trunk stabilization exercises

Lower-back exercises

Trunk strengthening and stabilization are key parts of any base program. Trunk strength should be developed prior to performing several lower-body and upper-body exercises.

The particular exercises you choose to perform will depend on your individual needs, goals, and personal program design. Here are some suggestions:

- Follow the routines provided in chapter 4 about program design. Start with the base program.

- If designing your own routines, be sure to select exercises for each body part so that your program trains the body in a balanced fashion.

- Strengthen any weak links prior to progressing to more challenging exercises.

- Read the description for each exercise prior to attempting any exercise. Pay close attention to the directions provided about proper alignment, positioning, motion, and technique.

- Always breathe during all resistance-training exercises. The standard breathing for most exercises is to inhale as the muscles lengthen and to exhale as the muscles contract.

If in doubt about the safety of any exercise, consult with a fitness professional and see a qualified physician before attempting the exercise.

TRUNK FLEX

TARGET MUSCLES: Rectus abdominis

JOINT MOTION: Trunk flexion

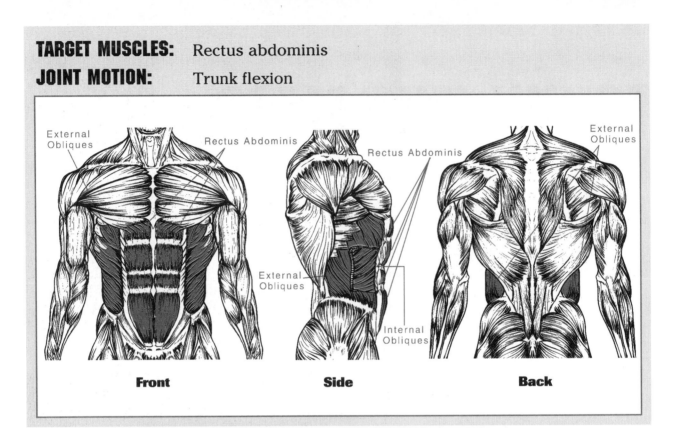

Front   **Side**   **Back**

EXERCISE DESCRIPTION

The Trunk Flex is a multiple-joint motion exercise designed to target the abdominals, particularly the rectus abdominis. Equal contractions from the obliques assist in providing a straight flexion of the trunk. Any combination of these muscular contractions can be performed to change which part of the abdominals will be targeted. Trunk flexion exercises can be performed at an inclined angle, flat, or at a declined angle, depending on the amount of resistance desired. Arm placement also will add or decrease resistance.

EXERCISE TIPS

- Keep the lower back pressed firmly against the back pad throughout the exercise.
- Work slowly, move one vertebra at a time, and keep tension in the abdominals.
- Keep the head and neck in a neutral position throughout the exercise.
- Try not to support the neck by placing the hands behind the head. Remember, the neck muscles are typically weak links and also need to be strengthened.

TRUNK FLEX

ALIGNMENT AND POSITIONING

1. Lie on an inclined, flat, or declined bench or platform with the back flat and the sacrum pressed firmly against the pad.

2. Place the legs on a chair, bench, or any object or brace the feet against a wall to create about a 45-90 degree angle between the trunk and legs.

3. Spread the legs apart so that the feet are pointed out at about two o'clock and 10 o'clock in order to limit hip flexor involvement.

4. Cross the arms over the chest and brace the hands under the chin to limit neck involvement.

TECHNIQUE

1. Contract the abdominals. Begin pulling the rib cage up and toward the pelvis, attempting to move only one vertebra at a time.

2. Continue to pull the rib cage up and toward the pelvis until the abdominals are fully contracted, keeping the sacrum pressed against the pad.

3. Hold, continue to contract the abdominals, and breathe out any remaining air.

4. Slowly lower the trunk one vertebra at a time back to its original starting position, never releasing the tension from the abdominals. Repeat.

RESISTA-BALL TRUNK FLEX

TARGET MUSCLES: Rectus abdominis

JOINT MOTION: Trunk flexion

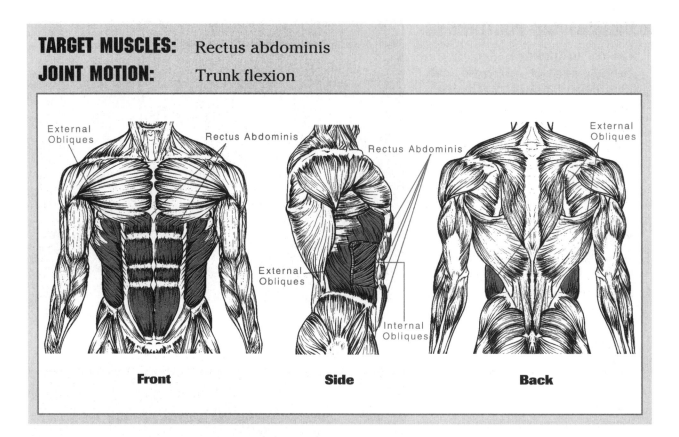

Front   Side   Back

EXERCISE DESCRIPTION

The Resista-Ball Trunk Flex is a multiple-joint motion exercise designed to target the abdominals, particularly the rectus abdominis. Equal contractions from the obliques assist in providing a straight flexion of the trunk. Performing trunk flexion on a Resista-Ball allows you to begin with the trunk in a slight degree of extension while still supporting the back, therefore increasing the range of resisted motion. Using the Resista-Ball also requires more internal stabilization than if exercising on the floor or on a bench, so it demands more from the obliques. Placement of the body and arms on the ball will determine the amount of resistance.

EXERCISE TIPS

- Keep the sacrum pressed firmly against the ball throughout the exercise, and avoid excessive hyperextension of the lower back.
- Work slowly, move one vertebra at a time, and keep tension in the abdominals.
- Keep the head and neck in a neutral position throughout the exercise.
- Try not to support the neck by placing the hands behind the head. Remember, the neck vertebrae are typically weak links and need strengthening too.

RESISTA-BALL TRUNK FLEX

ALIGNMENT AND POSITIONING

1. Lie on a Resista-Ball with the back slightly extended, the shoulders higher than the hips, and the sacrum pressed firmly against the ball.

2. Flex the knees to form approximately a 90-degree angle between the upper and lower legs.

3. Spread the legs, placing the knees just outside shoulder width.

4. Begin with the arms lightly supporting the head or crossed over the chest and hands under the chin to limit neck involvement.

TECHNIQUE

1. Contract the abdominals, and begin pulling the rib cage toward the pelvis. Attempt to move only one vertebra at a time.

2. Continue to pull the rib cage toward the pelvis until the abdominals are fully contracted, keeping the sacrum pressed against the ball.

3. Hold, continue to contract the abdominals, and breathe out any remaining air.

4. Slowly lower the trunk one vertebra at a time back to its original starting position, never releasing tension from the abdominals. Repeat.

REVERSE TRUNK FLEX

TARGET MUSCLES: Rectus abdominis

JOINT MOTION: Trunk flexion

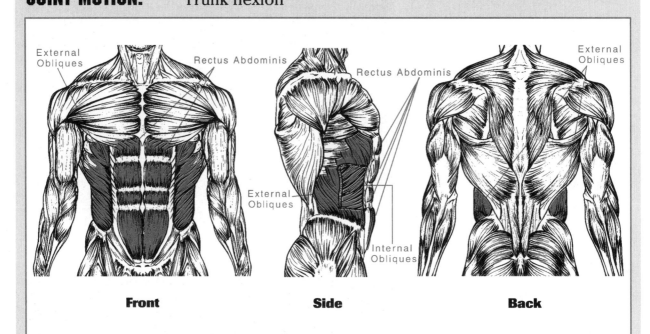

Front   **Side**   **Back**

EXERCISE DESCRIPTION

The Reverse Trunk Flex is a multiple-joint motion exercise designed to target the abdominals, particularly the rectus abdominis. Equal contractions from the obliques assist in providing a straight flexion of the trunk. Any combination of these muscular contractions can be performed to change which part of the abdominals will be targeted. Reverse trunk flex exercises can be performed at a declined angle, flat, or on an inclined angle, depending on the amount of resistance desired. Leg placement will also add or decrease resistance.

EXERCISE TIPS

- Keep the shoulder blades pressed firmly against the back pad or floor throughout the exercise.
- Avoid arching the back at any point.
- Work slowly, move one vertebra at a time, and keep tension in the abdominals.
- Keep the head and neck in a neutral position throughout the exercise.

REVERSE TRUNK FLEX

ALIGNMENT AND POSITIONING

1. Lie on a declined, flat, or inclined bench or platform with the back flat, shoulder blades and sacrum pressed firmly against the pad.

2. With the legs together, flex the hips and knees to form approximately a 90-degree angle or set them according to the desired resistance. (The further the legs are placed out away from the body, the greater the resistance.)

3. Hold firmly to the back or side of the bench, platform, or stationary object to anchor the upper body down.

TECHNIQUE

1. Contract the abdominals. Begin pulling the pelvis up and toward the rib cage, attempting to move only one vertebra at a time.

2. Continue to pull the pelvis toward the rib cage until the abdominals are fully contracted and the hips are rolled up slightly off of the pad.

3. Hold, continue to contract the abdominals, and breathe out any remaining air.

4. Slowly lower the trunk and hips one vertebra at a time back to their original starting position, never releasing the tension from the abdominals. Repeat.

RESISTA-BALL REVERSE TRUNK FLEX

TARGET MUSCLES: Rectus abdominis

JOINT MOTION: Trunk flexion

External Obliques

Rectus Abdominis

Rectus Abdominis

External Obliques

External Obliques

Internal Obliques

Front   **Side**   **Back**

EXERCISE DESCRIPTION

The Resista-Ball Reverse Trunk Flex is a multiple-joint motion exercise designed to target the abdominals, particularly the rectus abdominis. Equal contractions from the obliques assist in providing a straight flexion of the trunk. Reverse trunk flex exercises using a Resista-Ball force symmetrical contractions. They do not allow for much unequal pull from the abdominals or obliques without dropping the ball. Holding the ball with the legs also fixes the angle of the hips and limits the use of the hip flexors.

EXERCISE TIPS

- Keep the shoulder blades pressed firmly against the back pad or floor throughout the exercise.
- Avoid extending the back at any point.
- Work slowly, move one vertebra at a time, and keep tension on the abdominals.
- Keep the head and neck in a neutral position throughout the exercise.

RESISTA-BALL REVERSE TRUNK FLEX

ALIGNMENT AND POSITIONING

1. Lie on a declined, flat, or inclined platform with the back flat, shoulder blades and sacrum pressed firmly against the pad.

2. Place the legs over the ball with the legs slightly spread apart.

3. Hold firmly to a stationary object, or brace the arms on the floor in order to anchor the upper body down.

4. Begin with the head, legs, hips, and ball slightly off of the floor and with tension on the abdominals.

TECHNIQUE

1. Contract the abdominals and begin pulling the pelvis up and toward the rib cage. Attempt to move only one vertebra at a time.

2. Continue to pull the pelvis toward the rib cage until the abdominals are fully contracted with the hips rolled up slightly off of the pad.

3. Hold, continue to contract the abdominals, and breathe out any remaining air.

4. Slowly lower the legs and hips one vertebra at a time back to their original starting positions. Repeat.

RESISTA-BALL LATERAL TRUNK FLEX

TARGET MUSCLES: Internal obliques, rectus abdominis

JOINT MOTION: Trunk lateral flexion

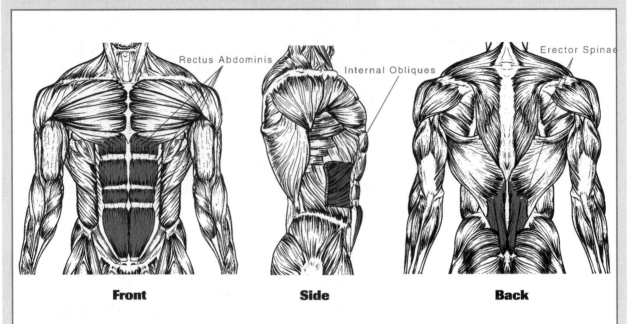

Front   Side   Back

EXERCISE DESCRIPTION

The Resista-Ball Lateral Trunk Flex is a multiple-joint motion exercise designed to target the internal obliques. Equal contractions from rectus abdominis and erector spinae assist in providing a straight lateral flexion of the trunk. They can be performed at an inclined angle, on a flat surface, at a declined angle, or on a Resista-Ball, depending on the amount of resistance desired. Arm placement will also affect the amount of resistance involved. Using a Resista-Ball allows for a greater range of resisted motion since the trunk can begin in lateral flexion to the opposite side. This is an advanced abdominal exercise so it is usually reserved for athletes interested in strengthening this motion for their particular sport.

EXERCISE TIPS

- Maintain a natural arch in the lower back. Avoid flexing or hyperextending.
- Work slowly, and keep tension in the obliques.
- Keep the head and neck in a neutral position throughout the exercise.

RESISTA-BALL LATERAL TRUNK FLEX

ALIGNMENT AND POSITIONING

1. Lie sideways on a Resista-Ball with the trunk laterally flexed over the ball and a natural arch in the lower back. (You may instead position yourself on the floor and place a pad or firm pillow just under the rib cage.)
2. Flex the knees, and spread the legs apart as far as needed to stabilize the body.
3. Begin with tension on the internal obliques with the arms overhead, crossed over the chest, or by the side, depending on the desired resistance.

TECHNIQUE

1. Contract the internal obliques, and begin pulling the side of the rib cage toward the side of the pelvis.
2. Continue to pull the rib cage toward the pelvis until the internal obliques are fully contracted. Keep a natural arch in the lower back.
3. Hold, continue to contract the internal obliques, and breathe out any remaining air.
4. Slowly lower the trunk back to its original starting position. Repeat.

TRUNK ROTATION

TARGET MUSCLES: External obliques

JOINT MOTION: Trunk rotation, trunk flexion

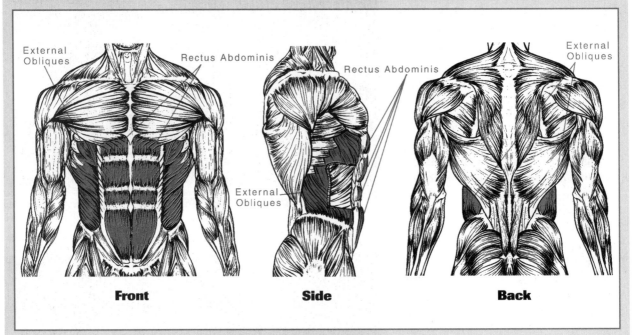

External
Obliques

Rectus Abdominis

Rectus Abdominis

External
Obliques

External
Obliques

Front   **Side**   **Back**

EXERCISE DESCRIPTION

The Trunk Rotation is a multiple-joint motion exercise designed to target the abdominals, particularly the external obliques. Due to the alignment of the external obliques, they tend to contract diagonally. Therefore, to target this muscle group properly, a certain degree of trunk flexion should accompany the rotation. Trunk rotation exercises can be performed at an inclined angle, flat, or at a declined angle, depending on the amount of resistance desired. Arm placement also will add or decrease resistance. This is an advanced abdominal exercise and is usually reserved for athletes interested in strengthening this motion for their particular sport.

EXERCISE TIPS

- Hold the pelvis and buttocks stationary once they have been originally positioned.
- Work slowly, and keep tension on the obliques and abdominals.
- Keep the head and neck in a neutral position throughout the exercise.

TRUNK ROTATION

ALIGNMENT AND POSITIONING

1. Place one hand on the side of the body opposite the legs and with the other hand lightly placed behind the ear so as to slightly support the head.

2. With the legs together, flex the hips and knees. Rest them on a chair, bench, or any object.

3. Rotate the hips and pelvis to one side while keeping the trunk and upper body straight.

4. Begin with shoulders slightly off the floor and tension on the abdominals.

TECHNIQUE

1. Contract the abdominals and obliques. Begin pulling the rib cage up and over toward the pelvis.

2. Continue to pull the rib cage toward the pelvis until the abdominals are fully contracted and the trunk and upper body are aligned straight with the angle of the pelvis.

3. Hold, continue to contract the abdominals and external obliques, and breathe out any remaining air.

4. Slowly lower the trunk back down and over to its original starting position. Repeat.

TRUNK RAISE (ABDOMINAL STABILIZATION)

TARGET MUSCLES: Iliopsoas, rectus femoris (with assisted abdominal stabilization)

JOINT MOTION: Hip flexion

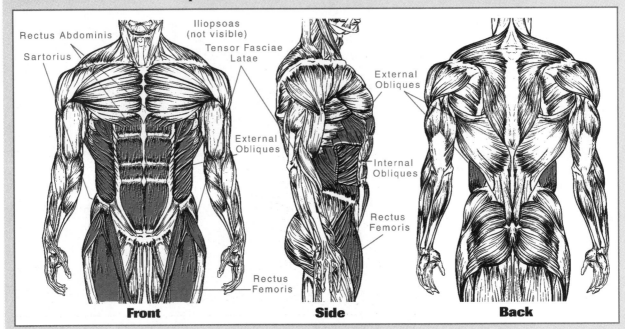

Front   Side   Back

EXERCISE DESCRIPTION

The Trunk Raise is a single-joint motion exercise designed to target the hip flexors. This exercise is classified as a trunk exercise due to the amount of effort exerted by the abdominal muscles to stabilize the trunk as it is being raised by the hip flexors. For most people, the abdominals are going to be far more challenged as stabilizers than the hip flexors are as primary movers. The abdominals' main role during most activities and primary function in everyday life is stabilization. Therefore, they should be trained as such. Trunk raises can be performed at an inclined angle, flat, or at a declined angle, depending on the amount of resistance desired. Arm placement will also add or decrease resistance.

EXERCISE TIPS

- Keep the trunk and back in a slightly flexed position throughout the exercise.
- Keep the legs close together, and avoid pulling too hard with the feet.
- Work slowly, and keep tension in the abdominals.
- Keep the head and neck in a neutral position or slightly flexed throughout the exercise.

TRUNK RAISE (ABDOMINAL STABILIZATION)

ALIGNMENT AND POSITIONING

1. Sit on a flat or declined bench with the trunk flexed and the feet anchored securely.

2. Flex the hips and knees. Keep both legs aligned straight and close together.

3. Begin with the upper body lowered just enough to provide tension on the abdominals, arms crossed over the chest, and hands braced under the chin.

TECHNIQUE

1. Slowly lower the upper body while keeping the trunk slightly flexed.

2. Continue to lower the upper body to the point where the trunk muscles are challenged to hold positioning.

3. Hold, continue to contract the abdominals and hip flexors, then slowly raise the trunk back to its original start position. Repeat.

LEG RAISE (ABDOMINAL STABILIZATION)

TARGET MUSCLES: Iliopsoas, rectus femoris (with assisted abdominal stabilization)

JOINT MOTION: Hip flexion

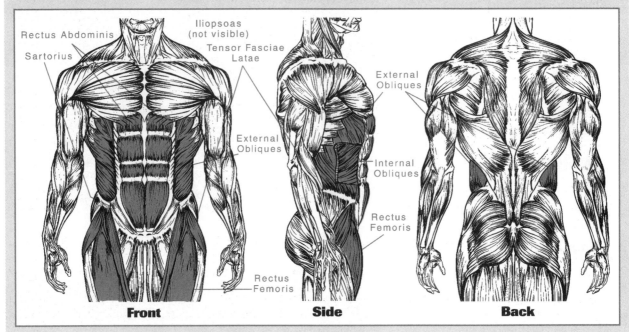

EXERCISE DESCRIPTION

The Leg Raise is a single-joint motion exercise designed to target the hip flexors. This exercise is classified as a trunk exercise due to the amount of effort exerted by the abdominal muscles to stabilize the trunk as the legs are being raised by the hip flexors. For most people, the abdominals are challenged far more as stabilizers than the hip flexors are as primary movers. Combining trunk stabilization exercises with active trunk exercises provides all-around strengthening and stabilization of the trunk. Leg raises can be performed at an inclined angle, flat, or at a declined angle, depending on the amount of resistance desired. Leg length will also add or decrease resistance. Begin with lifting only one leg before progressing to both.

EXERCISE TIPS

- Keep the trunk flat and the lower back pressed firmly against the pad throughout the exercise.
- Always begin the exercise with the legs up. Do not attempt to pull them up from a down position.
- Work slowly, and keep tension in the abdominals.
- Keep the head and neck in a neutral position or slightly flexed throughout the exercise.

LEG RAISE (ABDOMINAL STABILIZATION)

ALIGNMENT AND POSITIONING

1. Lay flat on an inclined, flat, or declined bench or platform. Press the sacrum, shoulder blades, and head firmly against the pad.
2. Hold lightly to the edge of the bench or a stationary object.
3. Flex the hips, and begin with one leg bent and one straight or both legs straight, and lowered just enough to provide tension on the abdominals. (Leg positioning will depend on hamstring flexibility).

TECHNIQUE

1. Slowly lower the leg(s) while keeping the back flat.
2. Continue to lower the leg(s) to the point where the trunk is challenged to hold the back down tight in its original position.
3. Hold, continue to contract the abdominals and hip flexors.
4. Slowly raise the leg(s) back to their original start position while pressing the lower back down firmly against the pad. Repeat.
5. To add resistance and stretch the calves, pull the toes back as far as possible.

HANGING LEG RAISE (ABDOMINAL STABILIZATION)

TARGET MUSCLES: Iliopsoas, rectus femoris (with assisted abdominal stabilization)

JOINT MOTION: Hip flexion (optional knee extension)

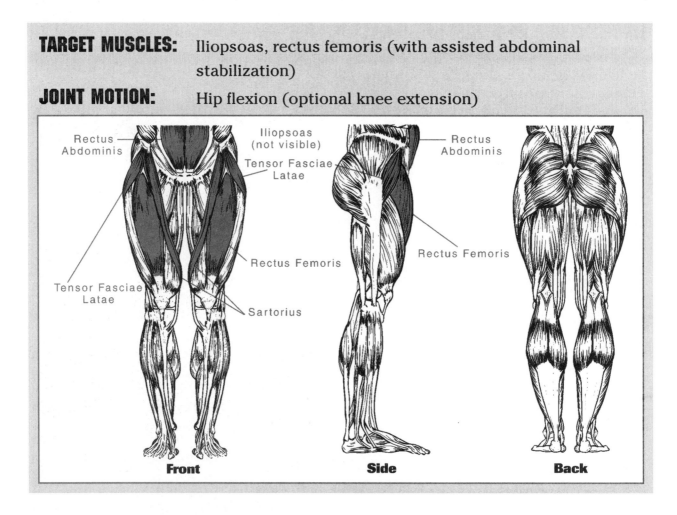

Rectus Abdominis — Iliopsoas (not visible) — Tensor Fasciae Latae — Rectus Abdominis — Tensor Fasciae Latae — Rectus Femoris — Rectus Femoris — Sartorius

Front   **Side**   **Back**

EXERCISE DESCRIPTION

The Hanging Leg Raise is a single-joint motion exercise designed to target the hip flexors. However, the vast amount of effort the abdominal muscles exert while attempting to stabilize the pelvis and spine makes this a very challenging exercise for the abdominals as well. Variations for decreasing or increasing the resistance are possible. For example, use one leg at a time to decrease intensity or perform the exercise with both legs extended straight to increase the intensity.

EXERCISE TIPS

- Keep the lower back pressed firmly against the back pad throughout the exercise.
- Keep the shoulder blades down and together throughout the exercise.
- Keep the head and neck in a neutral position throughout the exercise.

■ HANGING LEG RAISE (ABDOMINAL STABILIZATION)

ALIGNMENT AND POSITIONING

1. Stand on the lowest crossbars of the machine, and place elbows firmly on the pads.
2. Contract the abdominals. Flex the trunk and press the lower back firmly against the back pad.
3. Begin with the hips slightly flexed and the legs up just high enough to keep the lower back pressed against the back pad.

TECHNIQUE

1. Contract the hip flexors. Begin pulling the legs up slowly, keeping the back flat and the shoulder blades down.
2. Continue to pull the legs up until the upper legs are about parallel to the floor.
3. Hold, continue to contract the hip flexors while also contracting and stabilizing with the abdominals.
4. Slowly lower the legs to their original starting position, keeping the lower back flat. Repeat.

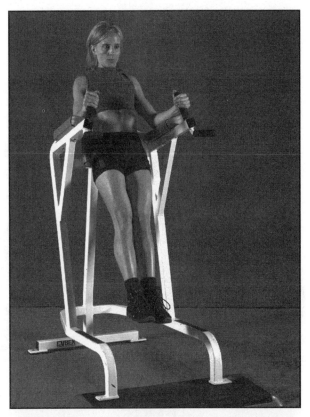

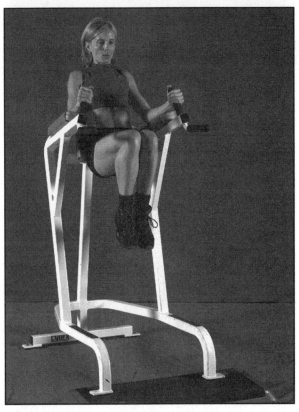

OPPOSITE ARM AND LEG RAISE

TARGET MUSCLES: Anterior deltoid, medial deltoid, gluteus maximus, hamstrings
(with assisted abdominal and erector spinae stabilization)

JOINT MOTION: Shoulder flexion, hip extension

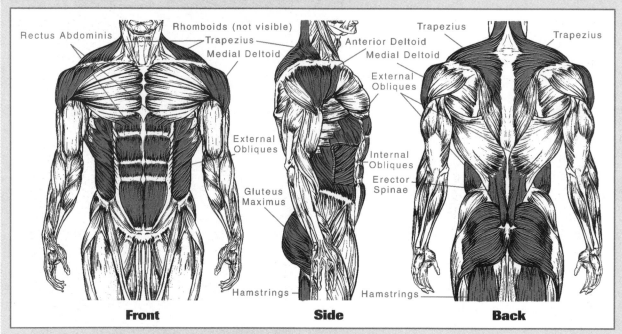

EXERCISE DESCRIPTION

The Opposite Arm and Leg Raise is a multiple-joint motion exercise designed to challenge the back and trunk muscles, particularly the erector spinae, as stabilizers. Though other muscle groups are responsible for moving the arm and leg, for most people, the muscles of the trunk are challenged far more as stabilizers than the other muscles are as primary movers. Combining trunk stabilization exercises with active trunk exercises provides all-around strengthening and stabilization of the trunk. This exercise can be performed with the trunk elevated on a pad or step, allowing the arms and legs to start at a lower position. It can also be done lifting just the arms, just the legs, lifting both the arms and legs, or any combination of these, depending on the desired resistance.

EXERCISE TIPS

- Keep the sternum and pelvis pressed firmly against the floor throughout the exercise.
- Avoid rotating, twisting, or hyperextending the spine in any way during the exercise.
- Work slowly and keep tension on the erector spinae and working muscles.
- Keep the head braced throughout the exercise.

OPPOSITE ARM AND LEG RAISE

ALIGNMENT AND POSITIONING

1. Lie prone on a pad or flat on the floor with one or both arms extended comfortably overhead, legs straight, and feet relaxed.

2. Rest the forehead on a towel or opposite arm, or turn the head to one side.

3. Begin with one arm and the opposite leg raised slightly off of the ground to provide tension on the deltoids, gluteus, and lower back.

TECHNIQUE

1. Start with the arm and opposite leg just off the floor, firmly pressing the sternum and pelvis against the pad.

2. Raise the arm and leg slightly, to the point where the back is challenged to hold the sternum and pelvis down tight against the pad.

3. Hold, continue to contract the muscles, then slowly lower the arm and leg to their original start positions. Repeat.

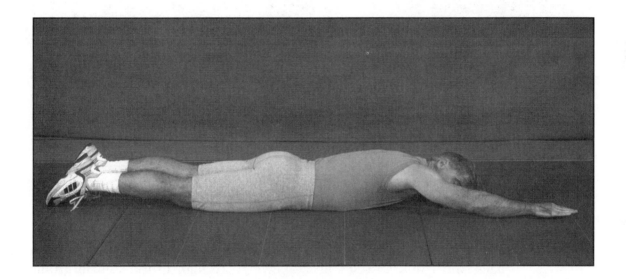

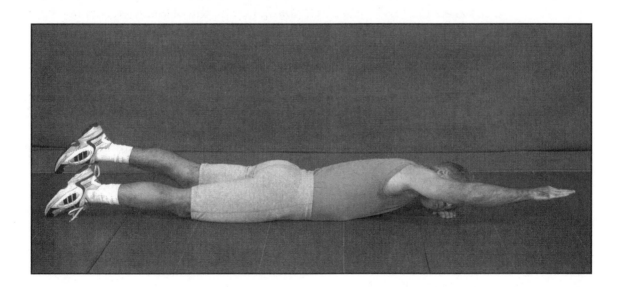

QUADRIPLEX (TRUNK STABILIZATION)

TARGET MUSCLES: Anterior deltoid, medial deltoid, gluteus, hamstrings
(with assisted abdominal and erector spinae stabilization)

JOINT MOTION: Shoulder internal rotation and flexion, hip extension

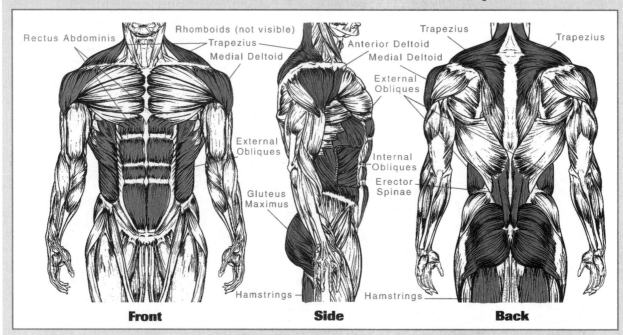

Rectus Abdominis — Rhomboids (not visible) — Trapezius — Medial Deltoid — External Obliques — Gluteus Maximus — Hamstrings — Anterior Deltoid — Medial Deltoid — External Obliques — Internal Obliques — Erector Spinae — Hamstrings — Trapezius — Trapezius

Front   **Side**   **Back**

EXERCISE DESCRIPTION

The Quadriplex is a multiple-joint motion exercise designed to challenge the back and trunk muscles as stabilizers. Though other muscle groups are responsible for moving the arm and leg, for most people, the muscles of the trunk are challenged more as stabilizers than the other muscles are as primary movers. Combining trunk stabilization exercises with active trunk exercises provides all-around strengthening and stabilization of the trunk.

EXERCISE TIPS

- Maintain a natural arch in the lower back, avoid flexing or hyperextending.
- Avoid rotating, twisting, or hyperextending the spine in any way during the exercise.
- Work slowly, and keep tension in the erector spinae and other working muscles.
- Keep the head and neck in a neutral position throughout the exercise.

QUADRIPLEX (TRUNK STABILIZATION)

ALIGNMENT AND POSITIONING

1. Get set on all fours in a ready position with a natural arch in the lower back.
2. Align the arms straight down from the shoulders with the elbows slightly flexed and the knees aligned directly under the hips.
3. Keep the head and neck in a neutral position.

TECHNIQUE

1. Begin with the arm and opposite leg straight out and slightly off the floor with tension on the deltoids, gluteus, and lower back.
2. Continue to raise the arm and leg to a level position or to the point where the back is challenged to hold a natural arch.
3. Hold, continue to contract the muscles, then slowly lower the arm and leg down to their original start positions. Repeat.

TRUNK EXTENSION (LOWER BACK)

TARGET MUSCLES: Erector spinae

JOINT MOTION: Trunk extension

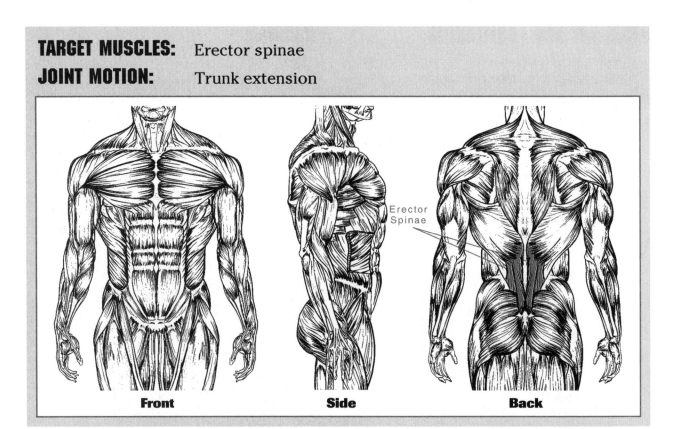

Erector Spinae

Front   **Side**   **Back**

EXERCISE DESCRIPTION

The Trunk Extension is a multiple-joint motion exercise designed to target the erector spinae. Trunk extension exercises can be performed at an inclined angle, flat, or at a declined angle, depending on the amount of resistance desired. Arm placement will also add or decrease resistance.

EXERCISE TIPS

- Keep the pelvis pressed firmly against the pad throughout the exercise.
- Avoid rotating, twisting, or hyperextending the lumbar spine any time during the exercise.
- Work slowly, and keep tension in the erector spinae.
- Keep the head and neck in a neutral position throughout the exercise.

TRUNK EXTENSION (LOWER BACK)

ALIGNMENT AND POSITIONING

1. Lie prone on an inclined, flat, or declined bench or platform with the legs slightly rotated out and the knees slightly flexed.

2. Place the arms next to the body, off to the side, or overhead, depending on the desired resistance.

3. Begin with the head and chest raised slightly off of the bench to provide tension on the lower-back muscles.

TECHNIQUE

1. Contract the erector spinae. Slowly raise the trunk. Pull the shoulder blades together and down toward the gluteus.

2. Continue to extend the back slowly, one vertebra at a time, to the point where the erector spinae is fully contracted without any spinal discomfort. (Muscle tightness is all that should be felt.)

3. Hold, continue to contract the erector spinae, then slowly lower the trunk back to its original start position. Repeat.

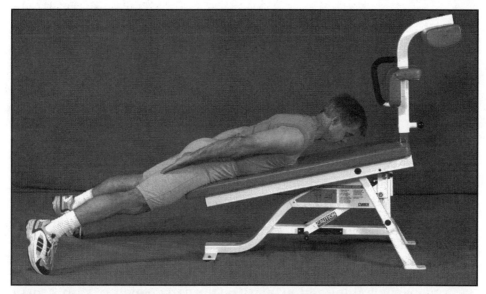

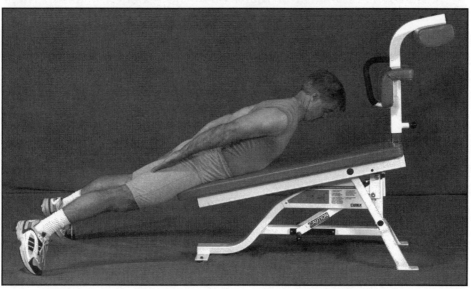

RESISTA-BALL TRUNK EXTENSION (LOWER BACK)

TARGET MUSCLES: Erector spinae

JOINT MOTION: Trunk extension

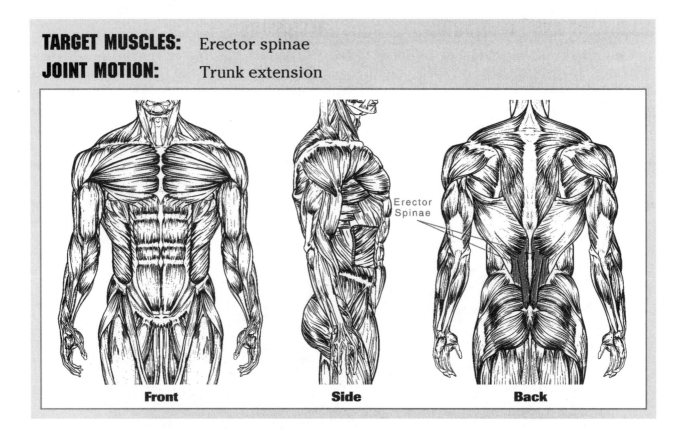

Erector
Spinae

Front   Side   Back

EXERCISE DESCRIPTION

The Resista-Ball Trunk Extension is a multiple-joint motion exercise designed to target the erector spinae. Performing the trunk extension on a Resista-Ball allows the trunk to begin in a position of flexion, therefore increasing the range of resisted motion. Because of its yielding surface, using a Resista-Ball requires more trunk stabilization than if on the floor, bench, or step. Arm placement will add or decrease resistance.

EXERCISE TIPS

- Keep the pelvis pressed firmly against the ball throughout the exercise.
- Avoid rotating, twisting, or hyperextending the lumbar spine at any time during the exercise.
- Work slowly, and keep tension in the erector spinae.
- Keep the head and neck in a neutral position throughout the exercise.

RESISTA-BALL TRUNK EXTENSION (LOWER BACK)

ALIGNMENT AND POSITIONING

1. Lie prone on a Resista-Ball with the knees slightly flexed and the legs spread out for balance.
2. Place the arms next to the body, off to the side, or overhead, depending on the desired resistance.
3. Begin with the trunk flexed yet with tension in the erector spinae.

TECHNIQUE

1. Pull the shoulder blades together and down toward the gluteus. Begin to contract the erector spinae slowly, extending the trunk one vertebra at a time.
2. Continue to extend the spine until the erector spinae are fully contracted without any spinal discomfort. (Muscle tightness is all that should be felt.)
3. Hold, continue to contract the erector spinae, then slowly lower the trunk back to its original start position. Repeat.

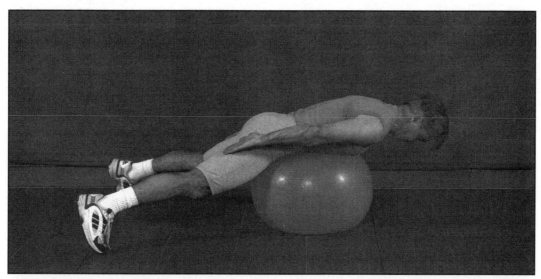

CHAPTER 6

LOWER-BODY EXERCISES

The following exercises are designed to target different muscles of the lower body. These exercises are not presented in any special sequence such as order of importance or suggested progression. They are presented in the following order for layout design and organizational reasons only.

Hip exercises

Compound-leg exercises

Upper-leg exercises

Lower-leg exercises

The particular exercises you choose to perform will depend on your individual needs, goals, and personal program design. Here are some suggestions:

- Follow the provided routines in chapter 4 on program design. Start with the base program.
- If designing your own routines, be sure to select exercises for each body part so that your program trains the body in a balanced fashion.
- Strengthen any weak links prior to progressing to more challenging exercises.
- Read the description for each exercise prior to attempting any exercise. Pay close attention to the directions provided about proper alignment, positioning, motion, and technique.
- Always breathe during all resistance exercises. The standard breathing for most exercises is to inhale as the muscles lengthen and to exhale as the muscles contract.

If in doubt of the safety of any exercise, consult with a fitness professional and see a qualified physician before attempting the exercise.

SEATED HIP FLEX

TARGET MUSCLES: Iliopsoas, rectus femoris

JOINT MOTION: Hip flexion

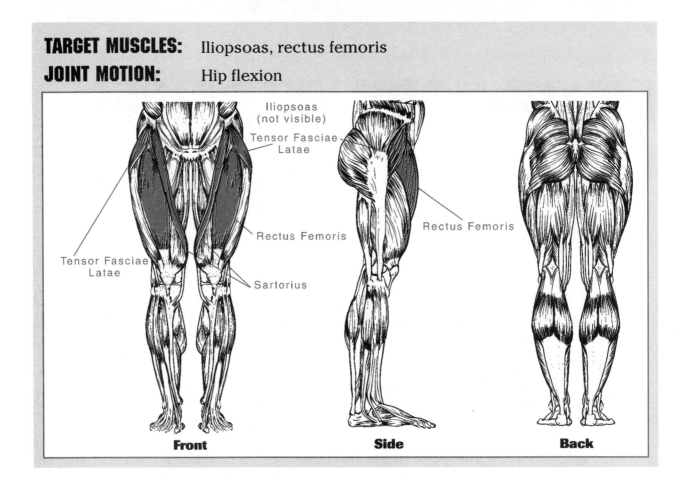

Iliopsoas (not visible)

Tensor Fasciae Latae

Rectus Femoris

Tensor Fasciae Latae

Sartorius

Rectus Femoris

Front   **Side**   **Back**

EXERCISE DESCRIPTION

The Seated Hip Flex is a single-joint motion exercise designed to target the hip flexors. Variations of this exercise can be done standing, leaning back against a wall, or sitting on the floor. Ankle weights, Exer-bands, cable machines, and other forms of resistance can be added if needed or desired.

EXERCISE TIPS

- Avoid twisting, rotating, or bending the leg during the exercise.
- Keep the shoulders back, a natural arch in the lower back, and the head and neck in a neutral position throughout the exercise.

SEATED HIP FLEX

ALIGNMENT AND POSITIONING

1. Sit on a bench or chair in a ready position with a natural arch in the lower back.
2. Place one foot flat on the floor with the leg bent in an approximate 90-degree angle.
3. Straighten the opposite leg, point the toe, and begin with the heel slightly off the floor.

TECHNIQUE

1. Contract the hip flexors, and begin pulling the leg up slowly, keeping it straight. Maintain a natural arch in the lower back.
2. Continue to pull the leg up as far as possible without bending the knee or losing spinal positioning.
3. Hold, continue to contract the hip flexors while stabilizing with the abdominals.
4. Slowly lower the leg to its original starting position. Repeat.
5. To add tension resistance and to stretch the calf muscle, pull the toes back as far as possible.

MACHINE STANDING HIP FLEX

TARGET MUSCLES: Iliopsoas, rectus femoris

JOINT MOTION: Hip flexion

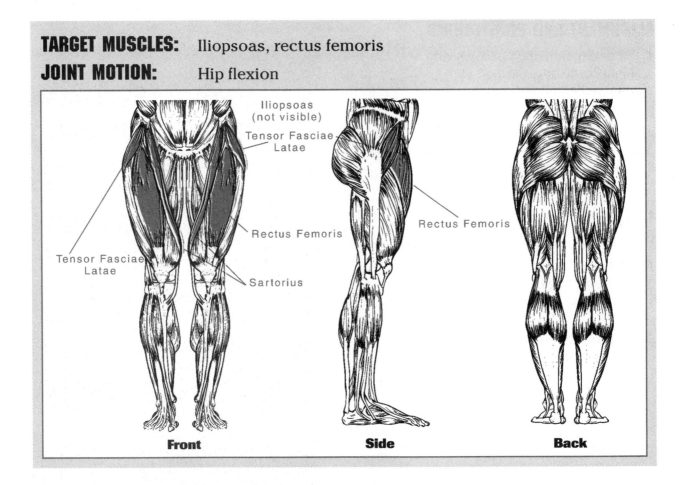

Front **Side** **Back**

EXERCISE DESCRIPTION

The Machine Standing Hip Flex is a single-joint motion exercise designed to target the hip flexors. However, as the hip flexors of the movement leg work against the resistance, the stationary leg and trunk muscles must support and stabilize the body. This demand makes the machine standing hip flex a better exercise for overall hip and pelvic stabilization than an exercise for the hip flexors.

EXERCISE TIPS

- Avoid twisting or rotating the leg, and relax the foot throughout the exercise.
- Keep the shoulders back and a natural arch in the lower back. Avoid rotating the pelvis in any way.
- Keep the head and neck in a neutral position throughout the exercise.

MACHINE STANDING HIP FLEX

ALIGNMENT AND POSITIONING

1. Stand in a ready position with the hip joint aligned with the axis of the machine and the pad placed just above the knee.
2. Hold the bar lightly with the arms straight and elbows slightly flexed.
3. Start with the inside leg against the pad and extended back about 10 degrees and with the weight suspended just off of the stack.

TECHNIQUE

1. Contract the hip flexors, and begin pulling the leg forward and up slowly.
2. Begin bending the knee, and continue to pull the leg up until the thigh is about parallel to the floor.
3. Hold, continue to contract the hip flexors while stabilizing with the trunk and stationary leg.
4. Slowly lower the leg to its original starting position. Repeat.

PRONE HIP EXTENSION

TARGET MUSCLES: Gluteus maximus, biceps femoris, semimembranosus, semitendinosus

JOINT MOTION: Hip extension

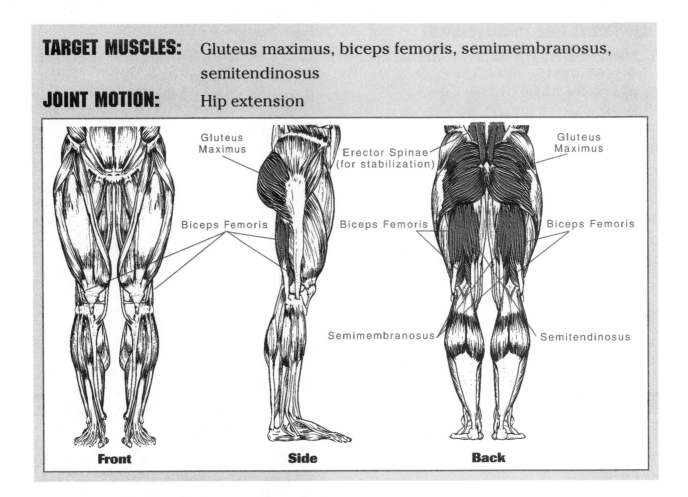

EXERCISE DESCRIPTION

The Prone Hip Extension is a single-joint motion exercise designed to target the hip extensors. Decreasing or increasing the resistance is possible. Examples include exercising one leg at a time or bending the legs to decrease the intensity, or performing the exercise with the legs straight and adding resistance to increase the intensity.

EXERCISE TIPS

- Keep a natural arch in the lower back. Avoid lifting the legs too high, causing the spine to hyperextend.
- Keep the head turned comfortably to the side and braced lightly against the bench.

PRONE HIP EXTENSION

ALIGNMENT AND POSITIONING

1. Lie prone on a bench with the axis of the hip joint directly over the end of the bench.
2. Hold the bottom of the bench securely. Press the chest and hips firmly against the pad while the head is turned to one side.
3. Straighten the legs. Have the feet pointed down and the toes just off of the floor.

TECHNIQUE

1. Contract the glutes and hamstrings. Begin pulling the legs up slowly, keeping them straight and the feet pointed down.
2. Continue to pull the legs up until the upper leg is about parallel to the floor.
3. Hold, continue to contract the glutes while stabilizing with the erector spinae.
4. You may now choose to rotate the hips externally by pointing the toes out while keeping the heels together. This will further contract the glutes and target the hip external rotators.
5. Slowly lower the legs to their original starting position. Repeat.

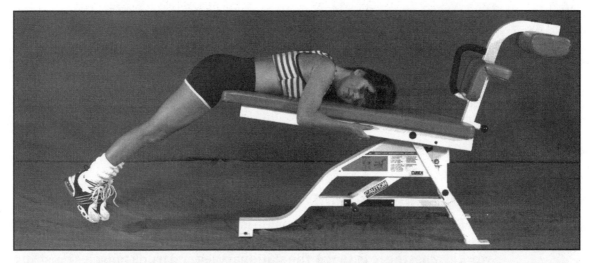

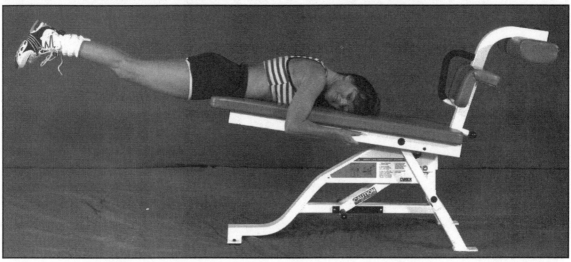

MACHINE STANDING HIP EXTENSION

TARGET MUSCLES: Gluteus maximus, biceps femoris, semimembranosus, semitendinosus

JOINT MOTION: Hip extension

Front   Side   Back

EXERCISE DESCRIPTION

The Machine Standing Hip Extension is a single-joint motion exercise designed to target the hip extensors. However, as the hip extensors of the movement leg work against the resistance, the stationary leg and trunk muscles must support and stabilize the body. This demand makes the machine standing hip extension a better exercise for overall hip and pelvic stabilization than an exercise for just working the hip extensors.

EXERCISE TIPS

- Avoid twisting or rotating the leg. Relax the foot throughout the exercise.
- Keep the shoulders back and a natural arch in the lower back. Avoid rotating the pelvis in any way.
- Keep the head and neck in a neutral position throughout the exercise.

MACHINE STANDING HIP EXTENSION

ALIGNMENT AND POSITIONING

1. Stand in a ready position with the hip joint aligned with the axis of the machine and the pad placed just behind and under the knee.
2. Hold the bar lightly, with the arms straight and elbows slightly flexed.
3. Start with the inside leg up at about a 90-degree angle from the body, knee bent, and with the weight just off of the stack.

TECHNIQUE

1. Contract the glutes and hamstrings, and begin pulling the leg slowly down and back.
2. Begin extending the knee, and continue to pull the leg back to approximately 10 degrees of extension.
3. Hold, continue to contract the hip extensors while stabilizing with the trunk and stationary leg.
4. Slowly raise the leg up to its original starting position. Repeat.

45-DEGREE HIP EXTENSION

TARGET MUSCLES: Gluteus maximus, biceps femoris, semimembranosus, semitendinosus

JOINT MOTION: Hip extension

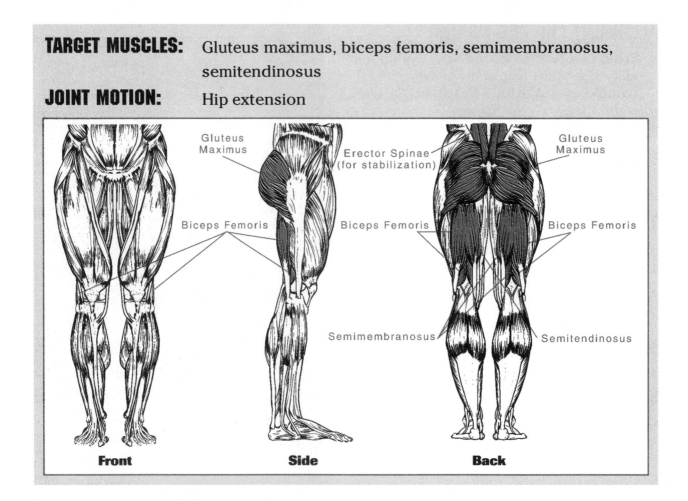

EXERCISE DESCRIPTION

The 45-Degree Hip Extension is a single-joint motion exercise designed to target the hip extensors. Because of the vast amount of effort the erector spinae muscles exert to stabilize the pelvis and spine, this is a very challenging exercise for the lower back as well. This could easily be classified as a lower-back stabilization type exercise as well as a hip exercise. The range of motion for this exercise depends on the degree of hamstring flexibility and the lower-back muscles' ability to stabilize the spine. Weight can be added to this exercise. However, due to the pressure against the knees, progressing to a standing hip extension may be better if more resistance is desired.

EXERCISE TIPS

- Keep shoulders back and a natural arch in the lower back throughout the exercise. Avoid flexing or hyperextending.
- Avoid twisting or rotating the legs, and keep the knees slightly bent during the exercise.
- Keep the head and neck in a neutral position throughout the exercise.

45-DEGREE HIP EXTENSION

ALIGNMENT AND POSITIONING

1. Stand on the platform of the machine with the legs and feet straight and aligned directly under the hips.

2. Adjust the pad to a position that is above the knee and where the top of the pad is just below the hip joint.

3. Set the spine in a ready position with the shoulder blades together and a natural arch in the lower back.

4. Keep a slight bend in the knees.

5. Place the arms behind the hips, crossed over the chest or out away from the body, depending on the desired resistance.

TECHNIQUE

1. Start to relax the glutes and hamstrings. Slowly begin to lower the upper body while maintaining spinal positioning and holding a natural arch in the lower back.

2. Continue to lower the upper body until you feel a light stretch in the hamstrings.

3. Hold, then contract the hamstrings and glutes and begin pulling the upper body up slowly.

4. Continue to pull the upper body up to the original start position while stabilizing with the erector spinae, then hold and squeeze the glutes together. Repeat.

BARBELL STANDING HIP EXTENSION

TARGET MUSCLES: Gluteus maximus, biceps femoris, semimembranosus, semitendinosus

JOINT MOTION: Hip extension

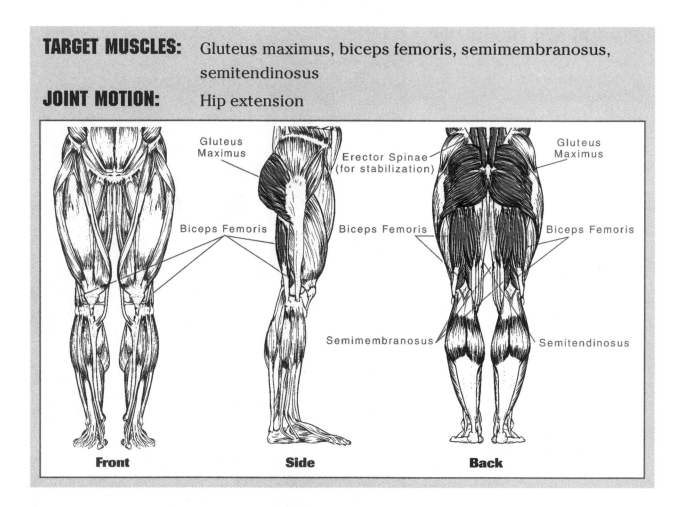

Gluteus Maximus

Erector Spinae (for stabilization)

Gluteus Maximus

Biceps Femoris

Biceps Femoris

Biceps Femoris

Semimembranosus

Semitendinosus

Front   **Side**   **Back**

EXERCISE DESCRIPTION

The Barbell Standing Hip Extension is a single-joint motion exercise designed to target the hip extensors. Because of the vast amount of effort the erector spinae muscles exert to stabilize the pelvis and spine, this is a very challenging exercise for the lower back as well. This could easily be classified as a lower-back stabilization type exercise. The range of motion for this exercise depends on the degree of hamstring flexibility and the lower-back muscles' ability to stabilize the spine. Begin this exercise as a stretch with no resistance until the lower back has been strengthened independently and the hamstrings have developed a good level of flexibility.

EXERCISE TIPS

- Keep shoulders back and a natural arch in the lower back throughout the exercise. Avoid flexing or hyperextending.
- Avoid twisting or rotating the legs, and keep the knees slightly bent during the exercise.
- Keep the head and neck in a neutral position throughout the exercise.

BARBELL STANDING HIP EXTENSION

ALIGNMENT AND POSITIONING

1. Stand with the legs aligned directly under the hips, knees slightly bent, and feet pointed straight ahead.
2. Hold on to a bar or dumbbell with the arms at a natural width just outside of the thighs.
3. Begin with the body standing in a ready position, shoulders back, and a natural arch in the lower back.

TECHNIQUE

1. Start to relax the glutes and hamstrings. Slowly begin to lower the upper body while maintaining spinal positioning and holding a natural arch in the lower back.
2. Continue to lower the upper body until you feel a light stretch in the hamstrings.
3. Hold, then contract the hamstrings and glutes, and begin pulling the upper body up slowly.
4. Continue to pull the upper body up to the original start position while stabilizing with the erector spinae. Hold and squeeze the glutes together. Repeat.

MACHINE SEATED HIP ADDUCTION

TARGET MUSCLES: Adductor magnus, adductor longus, adductor brevis, pectineus, gracilis

JOINT MOTION: Hip adduction

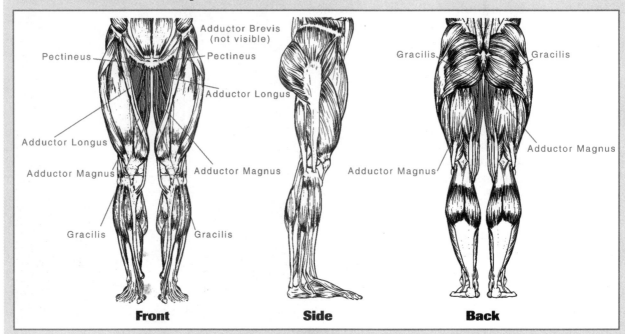

Pectineus — Pectineus
Adductor Brevis (not visible)
Adductor Longus
Adductor Longus
Adductor Magnus — Adductor Magnus
Gracilis — Gracilis
Front

Adductor Magnus
Side

Gracilis — Gracilis
Adductor Magnus — Adductor Magnus
Back

EXERCISE DESCRIPTION

The Machine Seated Hip Adduction is a single-joint motion exercise designed to target the hip adductors. Being in a seated position allows for approximately 90 degrees of hip flexion which is believed to promote a greater recruitment of the proximal adductors (the shorter adductors located closer to the hip). Standing, straight-leg versions do more to efficiently recruit the larger and longer adductors that extend through the thigh. The adductors also assist in hip extension type exercises such as squats, leg presses, and lunges.

EXERCISE TIPS

- Avoid twisting or rotating the legs or feet during the exercise.
- Avoid spreading the legs any wider than 45 degrees. (This is not a stretching exercise. Do not attempt to stretch any muscles when using an added resistance.)
- Keep the shoulders back, a natural arch in the lower back, and the head and neck in a neutral position throughout the exercise.

MACHINE SEATED HIP ADDUCTION

ALIGNMENT AND POSITIONING

1. Lean back or sit up on the machine, with the sacrum and shoulder blades pressed firmly against the back pad and a natural arch in the lower back. (Being able to sit up and away from the back pad depends on the ability to hold the spinal positioning throughout the exercise.)
2. Place feet flat and straight on the rungs of the machine with the upper leg parallel to the floor and in an approximate 90-degree angle.
3. Begin with the legs spread about 45 degrees apart and the weight suspended just off of the stack.

TECHNIQUE

1. Contract the hip adductors. Begin pulling the legs together slowly, keeping the feet straight ahead and relaxed.
2. Continue to pull the legs together as far as possible or until precisely when the lower lumbar region begins to flex.
3. Hold, continue to contract the hip adductors while stabilizing with the trunk muscles.
4. Slowly bring the legs back out to their original starting position. Repeat.

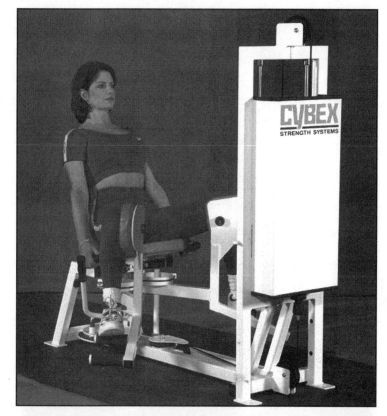

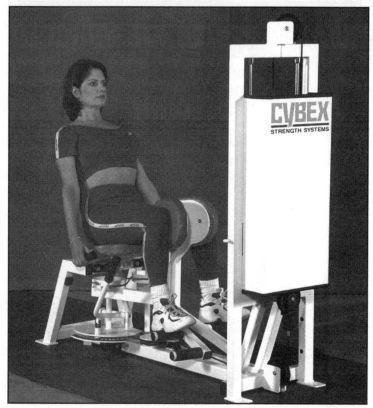

MACHINE STANDING HIP ADDUCTION

TARGET MUSCLES: Adductor magnus, adductor longus, adductor brevis, pectineus, gracilis

JOINT MOTION: Hip adduction

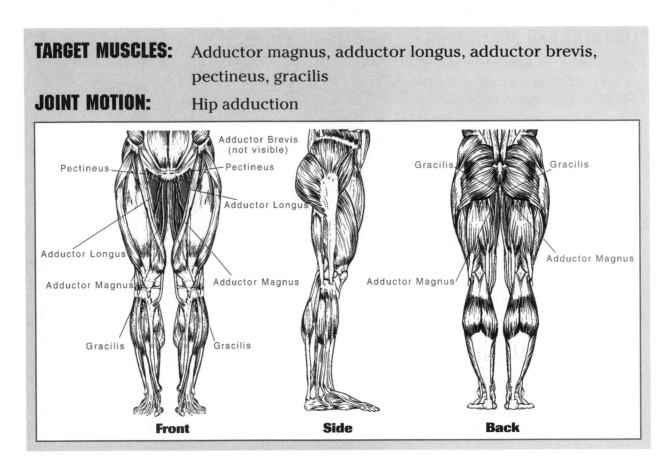

EXERCISE DESCRIPTION

The Machine Standing Hip Adduction is a single-joint motion exercise designed to target the hip adductors. However, as the hip adductors of the movement leg work against the resistance, the stationary leg and trunk muscles must support and stabilize the body. This demand makes the machine standing hip adduction a good exercise for overall hip and pelvic stabilization as well. Standing, straight-leg versions of this exercise do more to recruit the larger and longer adductors that extend throughout the length of the thigh than does the seated version. Hip adductors also assist with hip extension type exercises such as squats, leg presses, and lunges.

EXERCISE TIPS

- Avoid twisting or rotating the leg, and relax the foot throughout the exercise.
- Keep the shoulders back and a natural arch in the lower back. Avoid rotating the pelvis in any way.
- Keep the head and neck in a neutral position throughout the exercise.

MACHINE STANDING HIP ADDUCTION

ALIGNMENT AND POSITIONING

1. Stand in a ready position, facing and centered with the machine. Have the hip joint aligned with the level of the cam's axis.
2. Adjust the pad to just above the knee. Lightly hold the bars with the arms straight and elbows slightly flexed.
3. Start with the inside leg out at about a 45-degree angle from the body, leg straight, and foot pointed straight ahead with the weight just off of the stack.

TECHNIQUE

1. Contract the adductors, and begin pulling the leg in slowly.
2. Continue to pull the leg in until the thighs are together or as close as possible.
3. Hold, continue to contract the hip adductors while stabilizing with the trunk and stationary leg.
4. Slowly raise the leg out to its original starting position. Repeat.

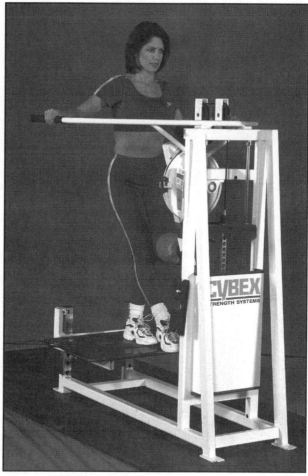

MACHINE SEATED HIP ABDUCTION

TARGET MUSCLES: Tensor fasciae latae, gluteus medius, gluteus minimus

JOINT MOTION: Hip abduction

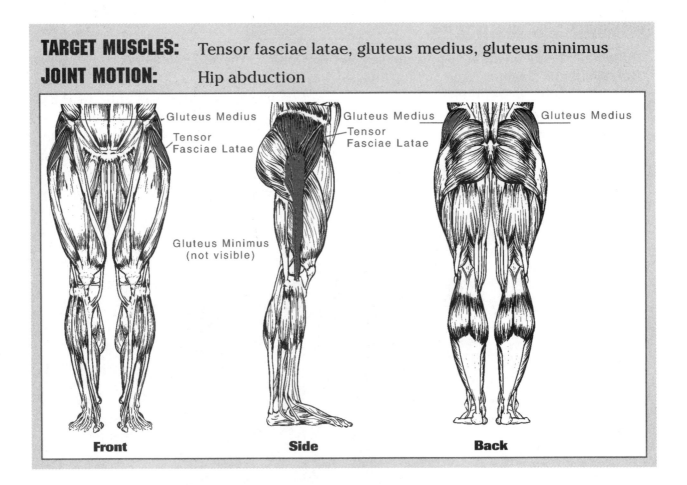

EXERCISE DESCRIPTION

The Machine Seated Hip Abduction is a single-joint motion exercise designed to target the hip abductors. Being in a seated position allows for approximately 90 degrees of hip flexion. This flexion is believed to promote a greater recruitment of the fibers of the longer abductor known as the tensor fasciae latae that runs down the length of the thigh. Standing, straight-leg versions of this exercise are more effective at recruiting the proximal and primary abductors known as the gluteus medius and gluteus minimus. Including some of both versions in your exercise program would be a good idea.

EXERCISE TIPS

- Avoid twisting or rotating the legs or feet during the exercise.
- Avoid spreading the legs any wider than 45 degrees.
- Keep the shoulders back, a natural arch in the lower back, and the head and neck in a neutral position throughout the exercise.

MACHINE SEATED HIP ABDUCTION

ALIGNMENT AND POSITIONING

1. Lean back or sit up with the shoulder blades and sacrum pressed firmly against the back pad and a natural arch in the lower back. (Being able to sit up away from the back pad depends on the ability to hold the spinal positioning throughout the exercise.)
2. Place feet flat and straight on the rungs of the machine with the upper leg parallel to the floor and in an approximate 90-degree angle.
3. Begin with the legs close together and the weight suspended just off of the stack.

TECHNIQUE

1. Contract the hip abductors. Begin pulling the legs apart slowly, keeping the feet straight ahead and relaxed.
2. Continue to pull the legs apart to about 45 degrees or as far as possible while keeping pelvic and spinal positioning.
3. Hold, continue to contract the hip abductors while stabilizing with the trunk muscles.
4. Slowly bring the legs back in to their original starting position. Repeat.

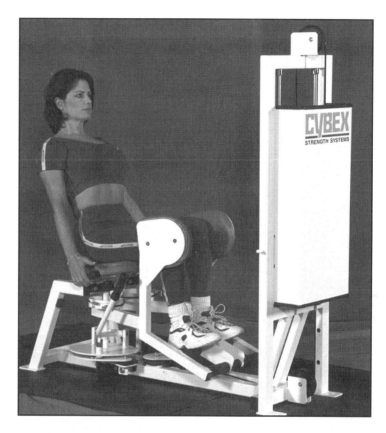

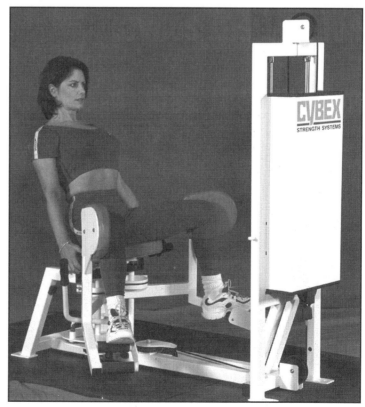

MACHINE STANDING HIP ABDUCTION

TARGET MUSCLES: Gluteus medius, gluteus minimus, tensor fasciae latae

JOINT MOTION: Hip abduction

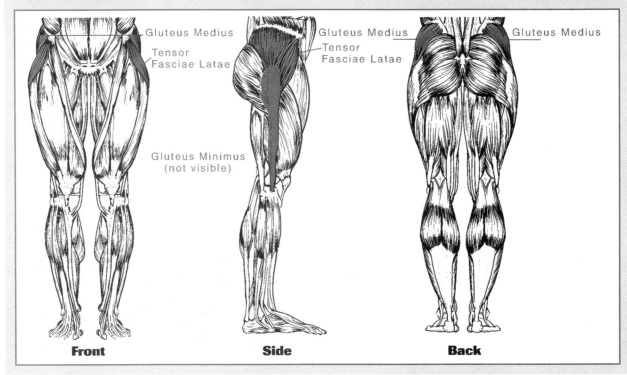

Gluteus Medius

Tensor Fasciae Latae

Gluteus Minimus (not visible)

Gluteus Medius

Tensor Fasciae Latae

Gluteus Medius

Front   **Side**   **Back**

EXERCISE DESCRIPTION

The Machine Standing Hip Abduction is a single-joint motion exercise designed to target the hip abductors. However, as the hip abductors of the movement leg work against the resistance, the stationary leg and trunk muscles must support and stabilize the body. This demand makes the machine standing hip abduction a good exercise for overall hip and pelvic stabilization as well. Standing, straight-leg versions of this exercise do more to recruit the fibers of the proximal and primary abductors known as the gluteus medius and gluteus minimus than does the seated version when the body is flexed at the hip. Including some of both versions in your exercise program would be a good idea.

EXERCISE TIPS

- Avoid twisting or rotating the leg, and relax the foot throughout the exercise.
- Keep the shoulders back and a natural arch in the lower back. Avoid rotating the pelvis in any way.
- Keep the head and neck in a neutral position throughout the exercise.

MACHINE STANDING HIP ABDUCTION

ALIGNMENT AND POSITIONING

1. Stand in a ready position, facing and centered with the machine, and having the hip joint aligned with the level of the cam's axis.
2. Adjust the pad to just above the knee. Lightly hold the bars with the arms straight and elbows slightly flexed.
3. Start with the movement leg aligned straight and slightly in front of the stationary leg, foot pointed slightly in, and weight just off of the stack.

TECHNIQUE

1. Contract the abductors, and begin pulling the leg out slowly.
2. Continue to pull the leg out to about a 45-degree angle or as close to it as possible while maintaining proper pelvic and spinal positioning.
3. Hold, continue to contract the hip abductors while stabilizing with the trunk and stationary leg.
4. Slowly lower the leg back to its original starting position. Repeat.

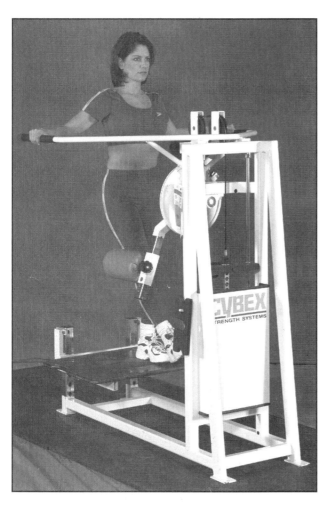
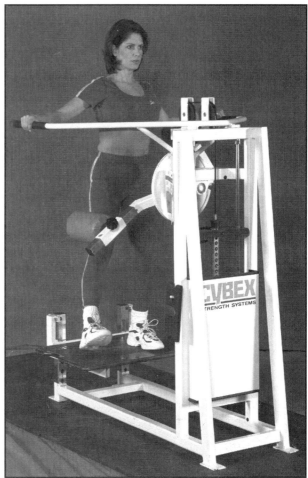

TUBING HIP INTERNAL ROTATION

TARGET MUSCLES: Gluteus medius, gluteus minimus, tensor fasciae latae

JOINT MOTION: Hip internal rotation

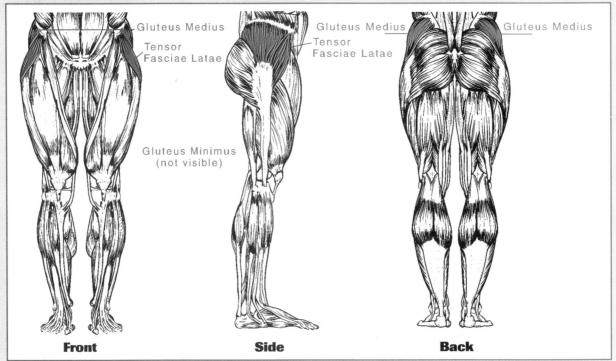

Gluteus Medius
Tensor Fasciae Latae
Gluteus Minimus (not visible)
Gluteus Medius
Tensor Fasciae Latae
Gluteus Medius

Front   **Side**   **Back**

EXERCISE DESCRIPTION

The Tubing Hip Internal Rotation is a single-joint motion exercise designed to target the hip internal rotators. Due to the difficulty of using free weights and lack of machines available for this joint motion, tubing, cables, and direct isokinetic resistance applied by a trainer are about the only way to provide the resistance. This exercise will help develop hip joint strength and stability and is an ideal base program exercise. Since the resistance is placed below the knee and will apply pressure at a lateral angle, this exercise should always be done with a light resistance. People with poor knee stability may wish to avoid this exercise or consult their physician prior to attempting it.

EXERCISE TIPS

- Keep a natural arch in the lower back, avoid flexing or hyperextending.
- Keep the legs from spreading farther apart or pulling closer together after their original positioning.
- Keep the head and neck in a neutral position throughout the exercise.

TUBING HIP INTERNAL ROTATION

ALIGNMENT AND POSITIONING

1. Sit up on a bench in a ready position with a natural arch in the lower back.
2. Spread the legs to about a 45-degree angle. Place one leg up on a pad or a towel so that it may freely rotate from side to side without the foot scraping the ground.
3. Begin with the hip externally rotated about 20 to 30 degrees (lower leg tilted in). Wrap the tubing around the foot or just above the ankle, providing a light tension.

TECHNIQUE

1. Contract the hip internal rotators. Begin pulling the lower leg out and across the front of the body to about 20 to 30 degrees of internal rotation without abducting or sliding the leg out.
2. Hold, continue to contract the hip internal rotators while stabilizing the body.
3. Slowly bring the leg back to its original starting position. Repeat.

TUBING HIP EXTERNAL ROTATION

TARGET MUSCLES: Gluteus maximus, piriformis, obturators, gemelli

JOINT MOTION: Hip external rotation

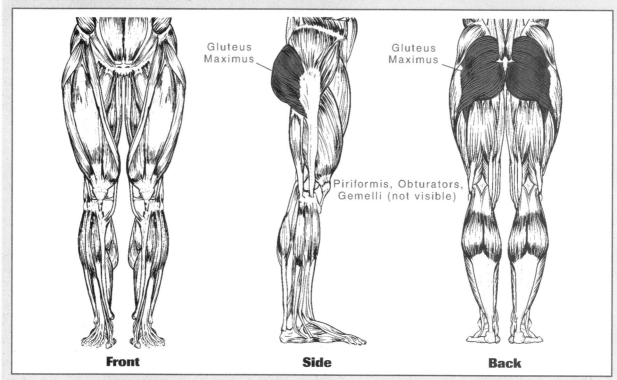

Gluteus Maximus

Gluteus Maximus

Piriformis, Obturators, Gemelli (not visible)

Front   **Side**   **Back**

EXERCISE DESCRIPTION

The Tubing Hip External Rotation is a single-joint motion exercise designed to target the hip external rotators. Due to the difficulty of using free weights and lack of machines available for this joint motion, tubing, cables, or direct isokinetic resistance applied by a trainer is about the only way to provide the resistance. This exercise will help develop hip joint strength and stability. It may be an ideal exercise to be included in a base program. Since the resistance is placed below the knee and will apply pressure at a lateral angle, this exercise should always be done with a light resistance. People with poor knee stability may wish to avoid this exercise or consult their physician prior to attempting it.

EXERCISE TIPS

- Keep a natural arch in the lower back, avoid flexing or hyperextending.
- Keep the legs from spreading farther apart or pulling closer together after their original positioning.
- Keep the head and neck in a neutral position throughout the exercise.

TUBING HIP EXTERNAL ROTATION

ALIGNMENT AND POSITIONING

1. Sit up on a bench in a ready position and with a natural arch in the lower back.

2. Spread the legs about 45 degrees apart. Place one leg up on a pad or a towel so that it may freely rotate from side to side without the foot scraping the ground.

3. Begin with the hip internally rotated about 20 to 30 degrees (lower leg tilted out). Wrap the tubing over the foot or just above the ankle, providing light tension.

TECHNIQUE

1. Contract the hip external rotators (glutes). Begin pulling the lower leg in and across the front of the body to about 20 to 30 degrees of external rotation without sliding the thigh inward.

2. Hold, continue to contract the hip external rotators while stabilizing the body.

3. Slowly bring the leg back out to its original starting position. Repeat.

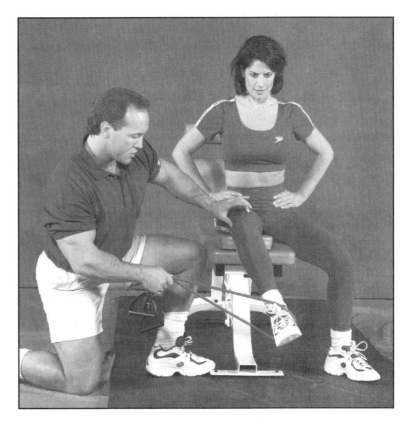

BODY WEIGHT SQUATS

TARGET MUSCLES: Gluteus, hamstrings, quadriceps

JOINT MOTION: Hip extension, knee extension

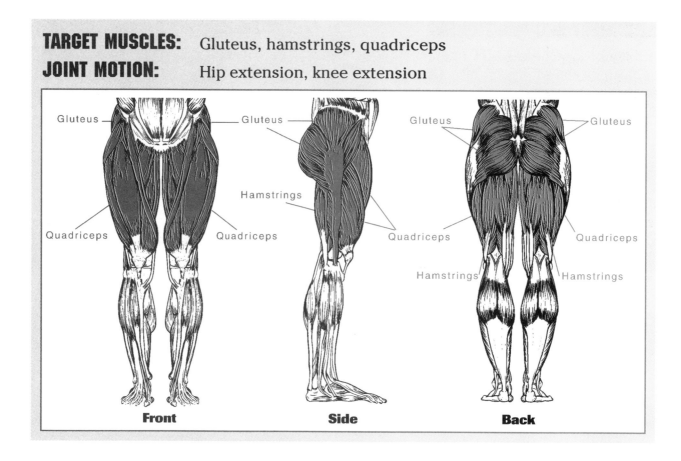

Front   Side   Back

EXERCISE DESCRIPTION

The Body Weight Squat is a multiple-joint motion exercise designed to target the hip and upper-leg muscles. Compound-leg exercises work more overall muscle than do other resistance-training exercises. The body weight squat provides much of the benefit of other types of squats but does not require the person to place any weight load on top of the back or directly through the spine. It is also a more functional exercise than other leg exercises because it more closely mimics movement we perform in daily life every time we sit or stand up.

EXERCISE TIPS

- Keep the weight over the ankles, and avoid having the heels lift off of the floor.
- Keep the knees aligned with the feet.
- Do not go any deeper than about the point when the upper and lower legs form a 90-degree angle and when the knees go past the toes.
- Keep the shoulders back, a natural arch in the lower back, and the head and neck in a neutral position throughout the exercise.

BODY WEIGHT SQUATS

ALIGNMENT AND POSITIONING

1. Stand in a ready position.
2. Position the legs slightly outside shoulder width and rotate hips and feet out about 20 to 30 degrees.
3. Begin with the hips and knees flexed, trunk in a slight forward lean, the spine in a ready position, and weight over the ankles.

TECHNIQUE

1. Bend the knees. Slowly begin to lower the body only to a point where the legs form an approximate 90-degree angle or only as far as you can while maintaining a natural arch in the lower back.
2. Hold, continue to contract the glutes, quads, and hamstrings, and stabilize with the trunk.
3. Contract the glutes and hamstrings. Slowly begin extending the legs, keeping the weight over the ankles.
4. Extend the legs back up to their original start position while maintaining proper spinal positioning. Repeat.

DUMBBELL SQUATS

TARGET MUSCLES: Gluteus, hamstrings, quadriceps

JOINT MOTION: Hip extension, knee extension

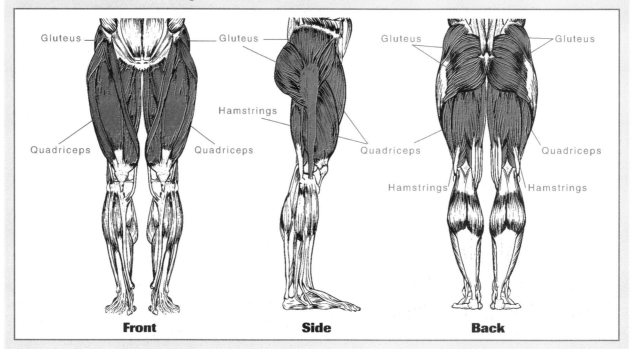

Front   **Side**   **Back**

EXERCISE DESCRIPTION

The Dumbbell Squat is a multiple-joint motion exercise designed to target the hip and upper-leg muscles. Compound-leg exercises work more overall muscle than do other resistance-training exercises. The dumbbell squat provides much of the benefit of other types of squats but does not require the person to place any weight load on top of the back or directly through the spine. It is also a more functional exercise than traditional squats because this exercise more closely mimics how someone may have to lift objects in daily life. Dumbbell squats may also be a good progression exercise after the person has mastered body weight squats but is not ready for free weight barbell squats or Smith Machine squats.

EXERCISE TIPS

- Keep the weight over the ankles, and avoid having the heels lift off of the floor.
- Keep the knees aligned with the feet.
- Do not go any deeper than about the point when the upper and lower legs form a 90-degree angle and when the knees go past the toes.
- Keep the shoulders back, a natural arch in the lower back, and the head and neck in a neutral position throughout the exercise.

DUMBBELL SQUATS

ALIGNMENT AND POSITIONING

1. Stand in a ready position. Hold a dumbbell in front of the body and between the legs with the arms straight and elbows slightly flexed.

2. Position the legs slightly outside shoulder width and rotate hips and feet out about 20 to 30 degrees.

3. Begin with the hips and knees flexed, trunk in a slight forward lean, the spine in a ready position, and weight over the ankles.

TECHNIQUE

1. Bend the knees. Slowly begin to lower the body only to a point where the legs form an approximate 90-degree angle or only as far as you can while maintaining a natural arch in the lower back.

2. Hold, continue to contract the glutes, quads, and hamstrings, and stabilize with the trunk.

3. Contract the glutes and hamstrings. Slowly begin extending the legs, keeping the weight over the ankles.

4. Extend the legs back up to their original start position while maintaining proper spinal positioning. Repeat.

BARBELL SQUATS

TARGET MUSCLES: Gluteus, hamstrings, quadriceps

JOINT MOTION: Hip extension, knee extension

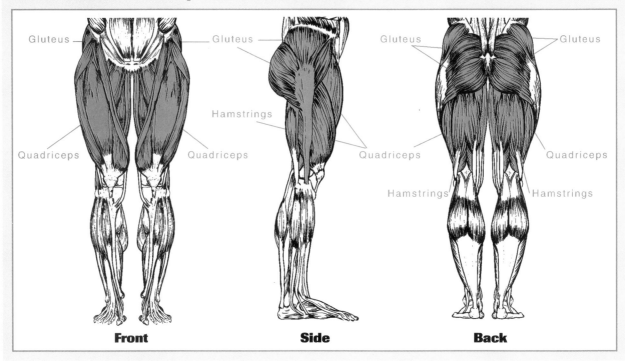

Front   **Side**   **Back**

EXERCISE DESCRIPTION

The Barbell Squat is a multiple-joint motion exercise designed to target the hip and upper-leg muscles. Compound-leg exercises work more overall muscle than do other resistance-training exercises. They require more work from the largest muscles of the body and so demand more effort. The barbell squat is a great leg exercise for most people when done properly. Do not get this exercise confused with the squats performed in the sport of power lifting. As with all of the compound-leg exercises, creating a 90-degree angle between the upper and lower legs is not necessary for the exercise to be of benefit. Everyone does not have the same optimum range of motion. Many people are not able to obtain that deep of an angle with proper form.

EXERCISE TIPS

- Keep the weight over the ankles, and avoid having the heels lift off of the floor.
- Keep the knees aligned with the feet.
- Do not go any deeper than about the point when the upper and lower legs form a 90-degree angle and when the knees go past the toes.
- Keep the shoulders back, a natural arch in the lower back, and the head and neck in a neutral position throughout the exercise.

BARBELL SQUATS

ALIGNMENT AND POSITIONING

1. Stand in a ready position. Place the bar just above the shoulder blades on the trapezius muscles.

2. Position the legs slightly outside shoulder width. Rotate the hips and feet out about 20 to 30 degrees.

3. Begin with the hips and knees flexed, trunk in a slight forward lean, spine in a ready position, and the weight over the ankles.

TECHNIQUE

1. Bend the knees. Slowly begin to lower the body only to a point that the legs form an approximate 90-degree angle or only as far as you can while maintaining a natural arch in the lower back.

2. Hold, continue to contract the glutes, quads, and hamstrings, and stabilize with the trunk.

3. Contract the glutes and hamstrings. Slowly begin extending the legs, keeping the weight over the ankles.

4. Extend the legs back up to their original start position while maintaining proper spinal positioning. Repeat.

SMITH MACHINE SQUATS

TARGET MUSCLES: Gluteus, hamstrings, quadriceps

JOINT MOTION: Hip extension, knee extension

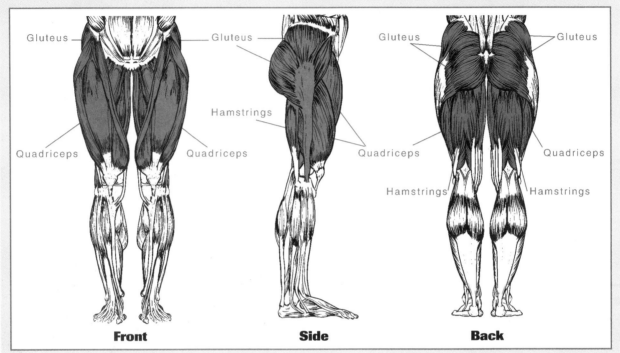

Front   **Side**   **Back**

EXERCISE DESCRIPTION

The Smith Machine Squat is a multiple-joint motion exercise designed to target the hip and upper-leg muscles. Compound-leg exercises work more muscles than other resistance-training exercises. They require more work and demand more effort. The Smith Machine squat should be performed similarly to a barbell squat. Before attempting this exercise, learn to squat outside of the smith machine so you will develop your balance and feel the correct motion. The Smith Machine should not be leaned against or used to change the positioning of the body. As with any compound-leg exercise, creating a 90-degree angle between the upper and lower legs is not necessary for the exercise to be effective. Not everyone's optimum range of motion is the same, and many people may not be able to obtain that deep of an angle with proper form.

EXERCISE TIPS

- Keep the weight over the ankles and avoid lifting the heels off the floor. Also keep the knees aligned with the feet.
- Do not go past the point when the upper and lower legs form a 90-degree angle and the knees go past the toes.
- Keep the shoulders back, a natural arch in the lower back, and the head and neck in a neutral position throughout the exercise.

SMITH MACHINE SQUATS

ALIGNMENT AND POSITIONING

1. Stand in a ready position. Place the bar just above the shoulder blades on the trapezius muscles.

2. Position the legs slightly outside shoulder width. Rotate the hips and feet out about 20 to 30 degrees.

3. Begin with the hips and knees flexed, trunk in a slight forward lean, spine in a ready position, and weight over the ankles.

TECHNIQUE

1. Bend the knees. Slowly begin to lower the body only to a point that the legs form an approximate 90-degree angle or only as far as you can while maintaining a natural arch in the lower back.

2. Hold, continue to contract the glutes, quads, and hamstrings, and stabilize with the trunk.

3. Contract the glutes and hamstrings. Slowly begin extending the legs, keeping the weight over the ankles.

4. Extend the legs back up to their original start position while maintaining proper spinal positioning. Repeat.

MACHINE LEG PRESS

TARGET MUSCLES: Gluteus, hamstrings, quadriceps

JOINT MOTION: Hip extension, knee extension

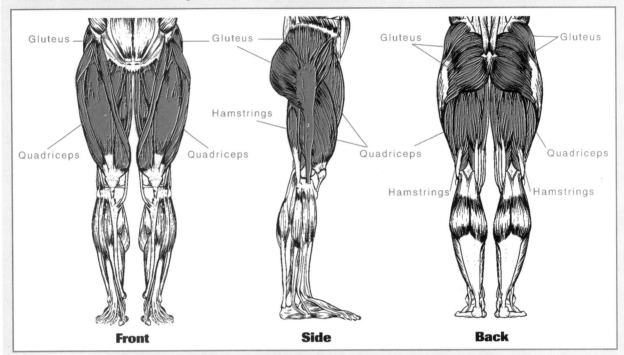

Front   **Side**   **Back**

EXERCISE DESCRIPTION

The Machine Leg Press is a multiple-joint motion exercise designed to target the hip and upper-leg muscles. Compound-leg exercises work more overall muscle than do other resistance-training exercises. The machine leg press provides much of the benefit of other compound-leg exercises without having to place the weight load on the back and through the spine. This may be an option for those individuals who are at an early stage of their fitness development or have not strengthened the trunk or stabilized the pelvis enough to perform other loaded, compound-leg exercises. People with certain back problems may also find this exercise a better alternative to leg exercises that require the back to support the resistance.

EXERCISE TIPS

- Avoid having the heels lift off of the platform or the sacrum lift off of the back pad.
- Keep the knees aligned with the feet.
- Try not to go any deeper than about the point when the upper and lower legs form a 90-degree angle.
- Keep the shoulders back, a natural arch in the lower back, and the head and neck in a neutral position throughout the exercise.

MACHINE LEG PRESS

ALIGNMENT AND POSITIONING

1. Adjust the back pad of the machine to provide comfort and allow for the maximum hip movement.

2. Lean back on the machine in a ready position, keeping the sacrum and shoulder blades pressed firmly against the back pad.

3. Rest the head against the back pad or use an additional pad if needed. (You may also stabilize it in a neutral position if you are able.)

4. Position the legs apart anywhere between 20 to 40 degrees, having the ankles aligned under the knees and the feet angled at the same 20 to 40 degrees as the legs.

5. Unlock the weight. Begin with the knees slightly flexed, buttocks pulled down, and a natural arch in the lower back.

TECHNIQUE

1. Bend the knees. Slowly begin to lower the legs until a 90-degree angle exists between the upper and lower leg, or only as far as possible while maintaining a natural arch in the lower back.

2. Keep the heels in contact with the platform, and feel a light stretch in the hamstrings.

3. Hold, continue to contract the glutes, quads, and hamstrings, and stabilize with the trunk muscles.

4. Pull the legs back up to their original start position while maintaining a proper spinal position. Repeat.

MACHINE HORIZONTAL LEG PRESS

TARGET MUSCLES: Gluteus, hamstrings, quadriceps

JOINT MOTION: Hip extension, knee extension

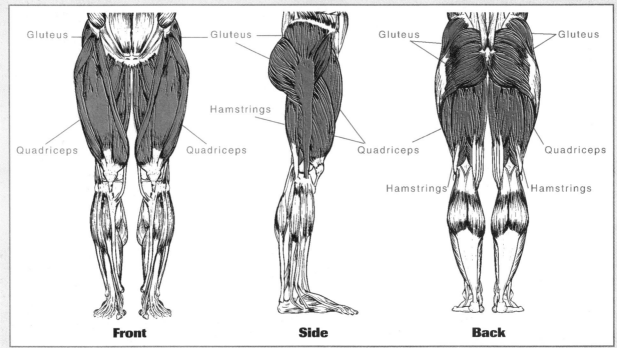

Front   Side   Back

EXERCISE DESCRIPTION

The Machine Horizontal Leg Press is a multiple-joint motion exercise designed to target the hip and upper-leg muscles. Compound-leg exercises work more overall muscle than do other resistance-training exercises. The machine horizontal leg press provides much of the benefits of other compound-leg exercises, but can be set to place less resistance through the spine. When lying horizontally, the gravity pull is perpendicular to the spine and the desired resistance is selected from the weight stack. The back pad limits the hips' natural movement and makes it difficult to hold proper spinal positioning and maintain the natural arch in the lower back when using heavier weight loads. Keep the resistance light for this exercise and progress to a squat when you are ready for more intensity.

EXERCISE TIPS

- Avoid having the heels lift off of the platform or the sacrum lift off of the back pad.
- Keep the knees aligned with the feet.
- Try not to lock the knees or go any deeper than about the point when the upper and lower legs form a 90-degree angle.
- Keep the shoulders back, a natural arch in the lower back, and the head and neck in a neutral position throughout the exercise.

MACHINE HORIZONTAL LEG PRESS

ALIGNMENT AND POSITIONING

1. Adjust the machine to begin with the hips and knees flexed to form approximately a 90-degree angle or as close to it as possible while being able to create a natural arch in the lower back.

2. Lie on the machine in a ready position with the sacrum and shoulder blades pressed firmly against the back pad.

3. Position the legs apart anywhere from 20 to 40 degrees with the ankles aligned under the knees and the feet angled at the same 20 to 40 degrees as the legs.

4. Tighten the glutes and legs, stabilize the spine, and begin with the weight just off of the stack.

TECHNIQUE

1. Slowly begin straightening the legs, keeping the weight over the ankles and a natural arch in the lower back.

2. Extend the legs to a straight position without locking the knees.

3. Hold, continue to contract the glutes, quads, and hamstrings, and stabilize with the trunk muscles.

4. Lower the body back to its original starting position while maintaining a proper spinal position. Repeat.

TRAVELING LUNGES

TARGET MUSCLES: Gluteus, hamstrings, quadriceps

JOINT MOTION: Hip extension, knee extension

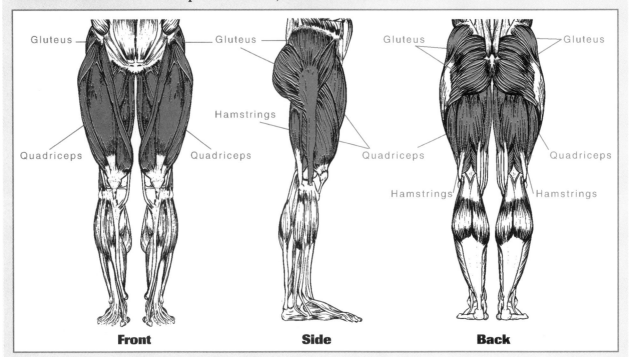

Front   **Side**   **Back**

EXERCISE DESCRIPTION

The Traveling Lunge is a multiple-joint motion exercise designed to target the hip and upper-leg muscles. Lunges are asymmetrical exercises that put the legs in front of and behind the body in different positions. Lunges are beneficial for those individuals and athletes looking to develop strength and stability in similar, asymmetrical positions. Lunges can place a lot of stress on the knees, particularly on the trail leg. Begin lunges only after good pelvic stability and overall leg strengthening have been accomplished.

EXERCISE TIPS

- Keep the pelvis level and under the shoulders with a natural arch in the lower back throughout the exercise.
- Keep the weight over the ankle of the lead leg.
- Keep the knee of the lead leg aligned with the foot and behind the toe.
- Keep the trail leg straight with the knee slightly flexed. Avoid pushing off with the trail leg.
- Keep the head and neck in a neutral position throughout the exercise.

TRAVELING LUNGES

ALIGNMENT AND POSITIONING

1. Stand in a ready position with legs aligned directly under the hips, feet pointed forward, and knees slightly flexed.

2. Place most of the weight onto the stationary or trail leg with the knee slightly flexed and the foot flat.

3. Keep the pelvis and hips level. Come up on the toe, and take most of the weight off of the moving or lead leg.

TECHNIQUE

1. Take a long stride forward with the lead leg landing softly on the heel. Keep the hips level and pelvis directly under the shoulders. Maintain proper spinal positioning.

2. Begin transferring the weight to the lead leg. Lower the body, keeping the trail leg straight and the knee slightly flexed.

3. Keep the weight over the ankle of the lead leg and the knee aligned with the foot.

4. Hold and balance, continue to contract the glutes, quads, and hamstrings, and stabilize with the trunk.

5. Keeping the weight over the ankle of the lead leg, pull the trail leg and body back up and forward to your original starting position. Repeat or alternate legs.

SMITH MACHINE REVERSE LUNGES

TARGET MUSCLES: Gluteus, hamstrings, quadriceps

JOINT MOTION: Hip extension, knee extension

Gluteus — Gluteus — Gluteus Gluteus

Hamstrings

Quadriceps   Quadriceps   Quadriceps   Quadriceps

Hamstrings

Hamstrings   Hamstrings

Front   **Side**   **Back**

EXERCISE DESCRIPTION

The Smith Machine Reverse Lunge is a multiple-joint motion exercise designed to target the hip and upper-leg muscles. Lunges are beneficial to those individuals and athletes looking to develop strength and stability in similar asymmetrical positions. Lunges can place a lot of stress on the knees, particularly the trail leg. Reverse lunges lower the stress by keeping most of the weight on the lead leg. The weight is never transferred to the trail leg. Lunges should be performed only after good pelvic stabilization and overall leg strengthening have been accomplished. A crane technique can be added to this exercise in order to further load the stationary leg and gluteus.

EXERCISE TIPS

- Keep the pelvis level and aligned under the shoulders, and a natural arch in the lower back throughout the exercise.
- Keep the knee of the lead leg aligned with the foot and behind the toe.
- Avoid going lower than the point when the lead leg forms a 90-degree angle.
- Keep the trail leg straight with knee slightly flexed and toes pulled back.
- Keep the head and neck in a neutral position throughout the exercise.

SMITH MACHINE REVERSE LUNGES

ALIGNMENT AND POSITIONING

1. Stand flat or on an elevated platform in a ready position with the shoulder blades together and the bar placed on the upper trapezius. (Using a step allows for the opportunity to safely increase the range of optimum motion.)

2. Align the legs directly under the hips with the feet pointed forward and the knees slightly flexed.

3. Begin with both feet on the platform, or one leg up in a crane position, with the weight on the stationary leg.

4. Keep the pelvis level and the back in a ready position.

TECHNIQUE

1. Step back with the trail leg, landing softly on the toe. Keep the weight on the lead leg, having the hips level and directly under the shoulders.

2. Continue to lower the body until the lead leg forms an approximate 90-degree angle. Keep the trail leg straight with the knee slightly flexed and a natural arch in the lower back.

3. Hold, continue to contract the gluteus and leg muscles of the lead leg, and stabilize with the trunk.

4. Keep the pelvis level and aligned under the shoulders. With the weight over the ankle, pull the leg and body back up to their original start position. Repeat.

MACHINE SEATED HAMSTRING FLEX

TARGET MUSCLES: Hamstrings, biceps femoris, semitendinosus, semimembranosus

JOINT MOTION: Knee flexion

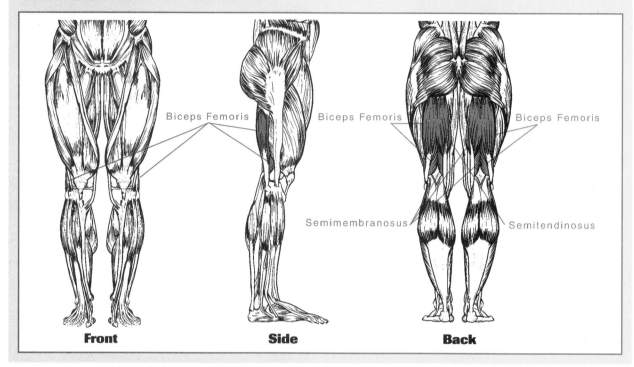

Biceps Femoris

Biceps Femoris

Biceps Femoris

Semimembranosus

Semitendinosus

Front   **Side**   **Back**

EXERCISE DESCRIPTION

The Machine Seated Hamstring Flex is a single-joint motion exercise designed to target the hamstrings. This seated version of a hamstring flex is a great alternative for people who have certain back problems, high blood pressure concerns, or other difficulties with using the prone type of machines for this exercise. However, this exercise has a decreased range of motion for many people in a seated position due to lack of hamstring flexibility.

EXERCISE TIPS

- Avoid twisting or rotating the lower leg, and keep the feet relaxed throughout the exercise.
- Avoid fully extending or locking the knees.
- Keep a natural arch in the lower back.
- Hold the shoulders back and the head and neck in a neutral position throughout the exercise.

MACHINE SEATED HAMSTRING FLEX

ALIGNMENT AND POSITIONING

1. Adjust the seat so that the knee joints are aligned with the axis of the machine. Adjust the leg pad so that it is just above the heels.
2. Lean back against the machine with the shoulder blades and sacrum pressed firmly against the back pad and a natural arch in the lower back.
3. Begin with the knees flexed and the weight just off the stack.

TECHNIQUE

1. Contract the hamstrings. Begin pulling the legs back slowly, keeping the lower legs straight and feet relaxed.
2. Continue to pull the lower legs back until they form an approximate 90-degree angle with the upper legs.
3. Hold, continue to contract the hamstrings while stabilizing with the trunk muscles.
4. Slowly bring the legs back out to their original starting position. Repeat.

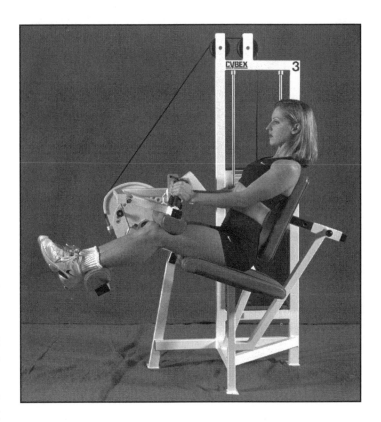

MACHINE PRONE HAMSTRING FLEX

TARGET MUSCLES: Hamstrings, biceps femoris, semitendinosus, semimembranosus

JOINT MOTION: Knee flexion

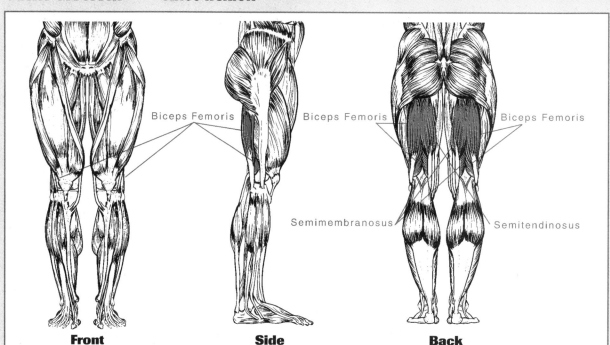

Front   Side   Back

EXERCISE DESCRIPTION

The Machine Prone Hamstring Flex is a single-joint motion exercise designed to target the hamstrings. This prone version of hamstring flex is a great alternative to the seated version for people who have limited hamstring flexibility. Lying down and taking a large amount of flexion out of the hips slackens the hamstrings, allowing for a greater range of motion for people with tight hamstrings.

EXERCISE TIPS

- Avoid twisting or rotating the lower legs, and keep the feet relaxed throughout the exercise.
- Avoid fully extending or locking the knees.
- Keep a natural arch in the lower back.
- Keep the head turned comfortably to the side and braced lightly against the bench.

MACHINE PRONE HAMSTRING FLEX

ALIGNMENT AND POSITIONING

1. Lie prone on a bench with the knee joints aligned with the axis of the machine and the pad adjusted just above the heels.

2. Hold securely onto the handles below the bench. Turn the head to one side, and firmly press the chest and pelvis against the pad.

3. Begin with the knees slightly flexed and the weight just off of the stack.

TECHNIQUE

1. Contract the hamstrings, and begin pulling the lower legs up slowly, keeping the pelvis pressed firmly down and lifting the knees slightly off the pad.

2. Continue to press the pelvis down and pull the lower legs up until they form an approximate 90-degree angle with the upper legs.

3. Hold, continue to contract the hamstrings, relax the feet, and stabilize with the trunk muscles.

4. Slowly lower the legs down to their original starting position. Repeat.

MACHINE QUAD EXTENSION

TARGET MUSCLES: Quadriceps (rectus femoris, vastus medialis, vastus lateralis, vastus intermedius)

JOINT MOTION: Knee extension

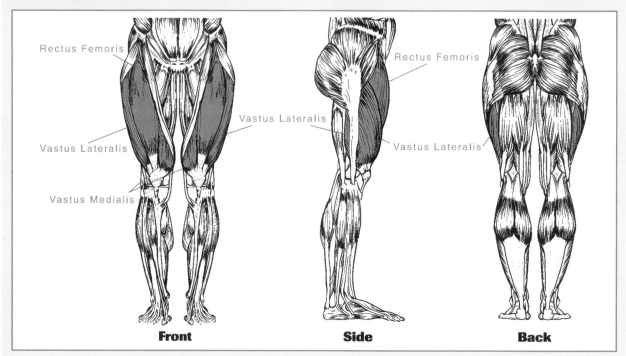

Rectus Femoris

Vastus Lateralis

Vastus Lateralis

Vastus Medialis

Rectus Femoris

Vastus Lateralis

Front   **Side**   **Back**

EXERCISE DESCRIPTION

The Machine Quad Extension is a single-joint motion exercise designed to target the quadriceps. Since knee extension is necessary for performing compound-leg exercises such as squats, leg presses, and lunges, and considering the amount of stress this exercise can place on the knee joint, this particular exercise may not be necessary or appropriate for some people to perform. If you choose to include this exercise in your routine, place it toward the end of your leg work. The quadriceps will be prefatigued, and you can use a lighter resistance.

EXERCISE TIPS

- Avoid twisting or rotating the hips or lower leg and keep the feet relaxed throughout the exercise.
- Avoid bringing the lower leg down past a 90-degree angle to the upper leg.
- Keep the shoulders back, a natural arch in the lower back, and the head and neck in a neutral position throughout the exercise.

MACHINE QUAD EXTENSION

ALIGNMENT AND POSITIONING

1. Adjust the seat so that the knees are aligned with the axis of the machine. Adjust the leg pad so that it is just above the feet.
2. Rotate the hips and roll the legs in to align the knees in a straight line with the hips.
3. Lean back against the machine with the sacrum and the shoulder blades pressed firmly against the back pad, and a natural arch in the lower back.
4. Begin with the lower part of the leg anywhere between a 10- and a 90-degree angle with the upper leg. (The amount of knee flexion will depend on the stability and condition of the knees and the goal of the individual.)

TECHNIQUE

1. Contract the quadriceps. Begin pulling the legs up slowly, keeping the foot relaxed.
2. Continue to pull the legs up until the knees are almost, but not fully, extended or only as far as possible while maintaining a proper spinal position.
3. Hold, continue to contract the quadriceps while stabilizing with the trunk muscles.
4. Slowly bring the legs back down to their original starting position. Repeat.
5. To increase resistance and stretch the calves, pull the toes back as you raise your legs.

MACHINE STANDING CALF EXTENSION

TARGET MUSCLES: Triceps surae (gastrocnemius, soleus)

JOINT MOTION: Ankle extension (also referred to as plantar flexion)

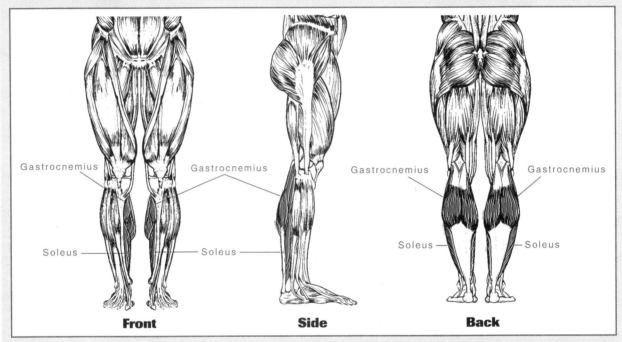

Gastrocnemius   Gastrocnemius   Gastrocnemius   Gastrocnemius

Soleus   Soleus   Soleus   Soleus

Front   **Side**   **Back**

EXERCISE DESCRIPTION

The Machine Standing Calf Extension is a single-joint motion exercise designed to target the triceps surae. When standing with the knee extended, the gastrocnemius takes the greatest amount of the load. When seated with the knee flexed, the gastrocnemius shortens, and the soleus is forced to bear more of the load. Including both versions of calf extension in your resistance-training programs is a good idea. This exercise is weight-bearing, so it can also help to develop increased spinal stability.

EXERCISE TIPS

- Avoid rotating the hips, and keep the feet pointed straight ahead throughout the exercise.
- Keep the ankles from rolling in or out.
- Keep the knees slightly flexed throughout the exercise.
- Keep the shoulders back, a natural arch in the lower back, and the head and neck in a neutral position.
- Try not to lower the heels much deeper than the ball of the foot or attempt to stretch the calves with weight.

MACHINE STANDING CALF EXTENSION

ALIGNMENT AND POSITIONING

1. Stand in a ready position with the feet pointed straight ahead and aligned directly under the hips.
2. Place the balls of the feet onto an elevated platform.
3. Begin with the heels just below the toes, tension on the calves, and the weight just off of the stack.

TECHNIQUE

1. Contract the calves. Begin pulling the heels up, keeping a slight bend in the knees and a natural arch in the lower back.
2. Continue to pull the heels up until the ankles are fully extended.
3. Hold, continue to contract the calves while stabilizing with the trunk muscles.
4. Slowly bring the heels and body back down to their original starting position. Repeat.

MACHINE SEATED CALF EXTENSION

TARGET MUSCLES: Triceps surae (gastrocnemius, soleus)

JOINT MOTION: Ankle extension (also referred to as plantar flexion)

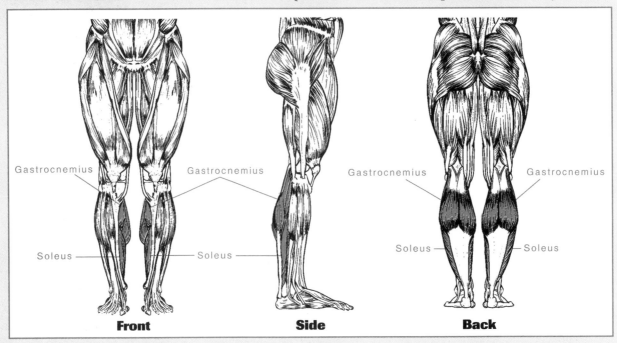

Front   **Side**   **Back**

EXERCISE DESCRIPTION

The Machine Seated Calf Extension is a single-joint motion exercise designed to target the triceps surae. When standing with the knee extended, the gastrocnemius takes the greatest amount of the load. When seated with the knees flexed, the gastrocnemius is shorter, and the soleus is forced to bear most of the load. Including both versions of calf extension in your resistance-training programs is a good idea.

EXERCISE TIPS

- Avoid rotating the hips, and keep the feet pointed straight ahead throughout the exercise.
- Keep the ankles from rolling in or out.
- Keep the shoulders back, a natural arch in the lower back, and the head and neck in a neutral position.
- Try not to lower the heels much deeper than the ball of the foot or attempt to stretch the calf with weight.

MACHINE SEATED CALF EXTENSION

ALIGNMENT AND POSITIONING

1. Sit in a ready position with the legs bent at an approximate 90-degree angle.
2. Point the feet straight ahead with ankles directly below the knees. Place the balls of the feet onto an elevated platform.
3. Begin with the heels just below the toes, tension on the calves, and the weight just off of the rack.

TECHNIQUE

1. Contract the calves. Begin pulling the heels up, keeping the ankles stable and feet pointed straight ahead.
2. Continue to pull the heels up until the ankles are fully extended. Lean slightly forward while maintaining proper spinal positioning.
3. Hold, continue to contract the calves while stabilizing with the ankles.
4. Slowly bring the heels and legs back down to their original starting position. Repeat.

TUBING TIBIALIS FLEX

TARGET MUSCLES: Tibialis anterior

JOINT MOTION: Ankle flexion (also referred to as dorsiflexion)

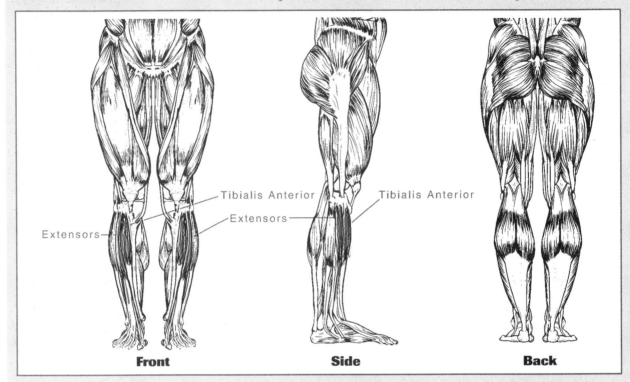

Front   Side   Back

EXERCISE DESCRIPTION

The Tubing Tibialis Flex is a single-joint motion exercise designed to target the ankle dorsiflexors, particularly the tibialis anterior. This is an important joint motion to include and also an important muscle to strengthen. It balances the amount of work performed by the calves in your exercise program and in other activities such as running and jumping. This exercise can also be performed using a specific machine, a cable machine, a DARD (dynamic axial resistance device), or a resistance directly applied by your trainer's hands.

EXERCISE TIPS

- Avoid twisting or rotating the legs. Avoid further bending or locking the knees throughout the exercise.
- Keep the ankles from rolling in or out.
- Keep the shoulders back, the lower back in a natural arch, and the head and neck in a neutral position.

TUBING TIBIALIS FLEX

ALIGNMENT AND POSITIONING

1. Sit in a ready position with one or both legs straight out from the body, the knees slightly bent, and the heels just off the end of the bench.

2. Begin with the toes below the heels as far as they are able to extend actively.

TECHNIQUE

1. Contract the tibialis anterior. Begin pulling the toes up and back, keeping the feet straight and knees slightly bent.

2. Continue to pull the toes up until the ankles are fully flexed.

3. Hold, continue to contract the tibialis anterior while stabilizing with the ankle.

4. Slowly bring the toes back down to their original starting position. Repeat.

CHAPTER 7

UPPER-BODY EXERCISES

The following exercises are designed to target different muscles of the upper body and are presented in the following order for layout design and organizational reasons, not in order of importance or suggested progression.

Chest exercises

Back exercises

Scapular exercises

Shoulder exercises

Upper-arm, biceps exercises

Upper-arm, triceps exercises

The particular exercises you choose to perform will depend on your individual needs, goals, and personal program design. Here are some suggestions:

- Follow the routines provided in chapter 4 about program design. Start with the base program.

- If designing your own routines, be sure to select exercises for each body part so that your program trains the body in a balanced fashion.

- Strengthen any weak links prior to progressing to more challenging exercises.

- Read the description for each exercise prior to attempting any exercise. Pay close attention to the directions provided for proper alignment, positioning, motion, and technique.

- Always breathe during all resistance-training exercises. The standard breathing for most exercises is to inhale as the muscles lengthen and to exhale as the muscles contract.

If in doubt about the safety of any exercise, consult with a fitness professional and see a qualified physician before attempting the exercise.

DUMBBELL CHEST PRESS

TARGET MUSCLES: Pectoralis major, anterior deltoid, triceps

JOINT MOTION: Horizontal shoulder adduction, elbow extension

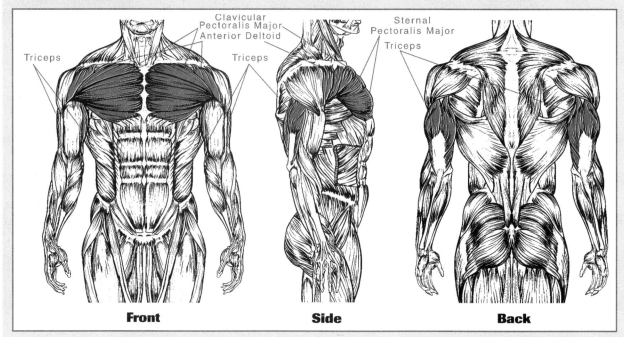

Front   **Side**   **Back**

EXERCISE DESCRIPTION

The Dumbbell Chest Press is a two-joint motion exercise used to target primarily the chest, particularly the sternal pectoralis major. Being a two-joint motion, this exercise also works the triceps and, typically, will allow you to safely use more weight than would the dumbbell chest adduction. Using dumbbells allows the lifter to bring the arms together as they come up. This provides the chest with a greater contraction than could be accomplished using a barbell or most chest press type machines.

EXERCISE TIPS

- Keep the feet planted flat and the sacrum pressed firmly onto the bench.
- Avoid lowering the arms any deeper than when they are parallel to the floor.
- Avoid rotating the shoulders or bending the wrists.
- Keep the shoulder blades together and a natural arch in the lower back throughout the exercise.

DUMBBELL CHEST PRESS

ALIGNMENT AND POSITIONING

1. Plant the feet firmly onto the floor or an elevated platform.
2. Place the sacrum, head, and shoulder blades firmly onto the bench, keeping a natural arch in the lower back.
3. Pull the shoulder blades tightly together, and hold them there throughout the exercise (scapular retraction).
4. Align the arms straight up from the shoulders, elbows slightly flexed and rotated out. Position the hands and dumbbells perpendicular to the body.

TECHNIQUE

1. Bend the elbows. Lower the arms to about 90 degrees from the body or parallel to the ground without rotating the shoulders.
2. Hold, then contract the chest, and pull the arms up and together to their original starting position without locking the elbows or rotating the shoulders.
3. Keep the chest tight at the finish of each repetition. Repeat.

BARBELL CHEST PRESS

TARGET MUSCLES: Pectoralis major, anterior deltoid, triceps

JOINT MOTION: Horizontal adduction, elbow extension

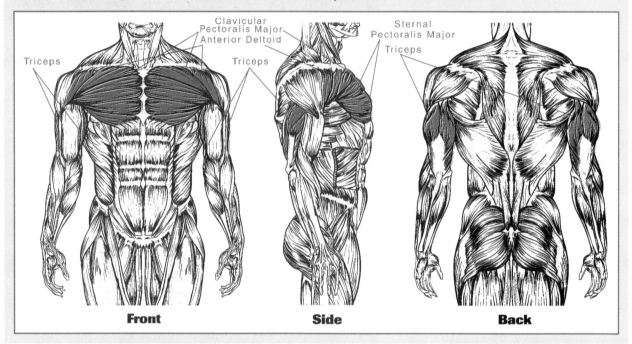

EXERCISE DESCRIPTION

The Barbell Chest Press is a two-joint motion designed to target primarily the chest muscles, particularly the sternal pectoralis major. By using a barbell, most people can balance and control the weight more easily than they could with dumbbells. This also enables most people to handle a greater total weight load. However, using a barbell instead of dumbbells prohibits full adduction of the arms and limits the joints' range of motion. Therefore, the barbell chest press is not as efficient an exercise for the chest. The technique presented here is designed with the goal of training the chest. This is different from the traditional bench press techniques used for power-lifting competitions where the goal is to move the weight.

EXERCISE TIPS

- Keep the feet planted flat, and the head and sacrum pressed firmly against the bench.
- Avoid lowering the arms any deeper than when they are parallel to the floor.
- Avoid rotating the shoulders or bending the wrists.
- Keep the shoulder blades down and together and a natural arch in the lower back throughout the exercise.

BARBELL CHEST PRESS

ALIGNMENT AND POSITIONING

1. Plant the feet firmly onto the floor or an elevated platform.

2. Place the sacrum, head, and shoulder blades firmly onto the bench, keeping a natural arch in the lower back.

3. Pull the shoulder blades tightly together, and hold them there throughout the exercise (scapular retraction).

4. Place the hands outside the shoulders so that the elbow will form approximately a 90-degree angle when the upper arms are parallel to the floor.

TECHNIQUE

1. Bend the elbows. Lower the arms down to about 90 degrees from the body or parallel to the ground without rotating the shoulders.

2. Hold, then contract the chest, and pull the arms up and together to their original starting position without locking the elbows or rotating the shoulders.

3. Keep the chest tight at the finish of each repetition. Repeat.

MACHINE CHEST PRESS

TARGET MUSCLES: Pectoralis major, anterior deltoid, triceps

JOINT MOTION: Horizontal adduction, elbow extension

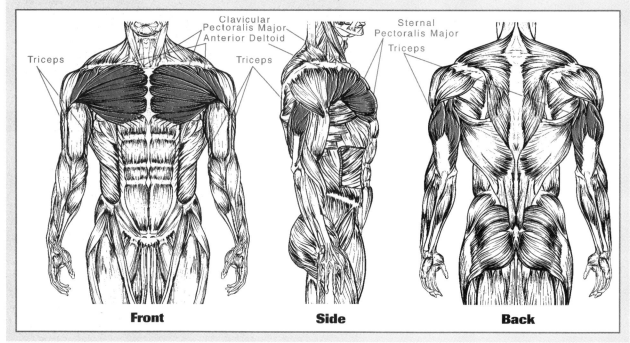

Front   Side   Back

EXERCISE DESCRIPTION

The Machine Chest Press is another two-joint motion exercise designed to target the chest muscles, primarily the sternal pectoralis major. A machine chest press provides much more balance and control than do free weights. This can be either a benefit or a limitation, depending on your goal for using this piece of equipment. However, the form and technique should be very similar to that when using a barbell. Like the barbell chest press, you cannot fully adduct the arms in a machine chest press. Similar machines are available with incline angles that will target more of the clavicular pectoralis major.

EXERCISE TIPS

- Keep the feet flat and the sacrum pressed firmly against the bench.
- Keep the arms horizontal or parallel to the floor.
- Avoid taking the upper arms any farther back than when the elbows are straight out to the side of the body.
- Keep the shoulder blades down and together and a natural arch in the lower back throughout the exercise.
- Keep the head and neck in a neutral position throughout the exercise.

MACHINE CHEST PRESS

ALIGNMENT AND POSITIONING

1. Plant the feet firmly onto the floor or braced on the machine.
2. Set the seat height to allow the arms to be about parallel to the floor when holding the horizontal set of handles.
3. Place the sacrum, shoulder blades, and head firmly against the bench, keeping a natural arch in the lower back.
4. Pull the shoulder blades tightly together, and hold them there throughout the exercise (scapular retraction).
5. Use the foot pedal or have a partner start with the weight out so that the arms are straight but not locked, the elbows are rotated out, and the wrists are in neutral.

TECHNIQUE

1. Bend the elbows. Begin bringing the arms back, keeping them horizontal with the elbows and aligned with the wrists.
2. Continue to bring the arms back until the upper arms are almost straight out to the side of the body.
3. Contract the chest, and push the arms forward all the way back to the original start position.
4. Keep the chest tight, scapulae retracted, and the elbows slightly flexed at the finish of each repetition. Repeat.

DUMBBELL INCLINE CHEST PRESS

TARGET MUSCLES: Pectoralis major, anterior deltoid, triceps

JOINT MOTION: Horizontal adduction, elbow extension

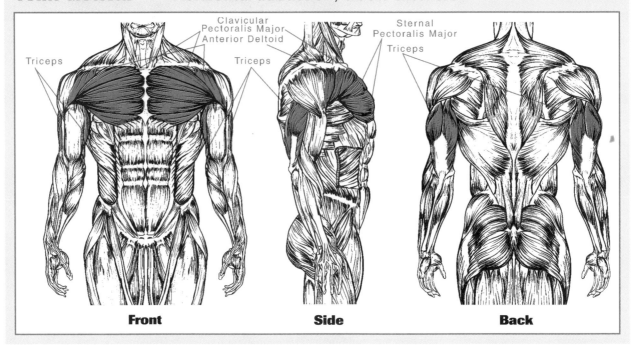

Front   Side   Back

EXERCISE DESCRIPTION

The Dumbbell Incline Chest Press is a two-joint motion exercise designed to target the upper chest and anterior deltoids, particularly the clavicular pectoralis major. The greater the incline angle, the less the sternal pectoralis muscle fibers are able to assist and the more the clavicular pectoralis and anterior deltoid fibers are used. The incline can continue to be elevated to a position where the anterior deltoid becomes the main target muscle. We then refer to this exercise as a dumbbell front delt press.

EXERCISE TIPS

- Keep the feet planted flat, and the head and sacrum pressed firmly onto the bench.
- Avoid lowering the arms any deeper than when they are parallel to the ground.
- Avoid rotating the shoulders or bending the wrists.
- Keep the shoulder blades together and a natural arch in the lower back throughout the exercise.

DUMBBELL INCLINE CHEST PRESS

ALIGNMENT AND POSITIONING

1. Plant the feet firmly onto the floor or an elevated platform.
2. Place the sacrum, head, and shoulder blades firmly onto the bench, keeping a natural arch in the lower back.
3. Pull the shoulder blades tightly together, and hold them throughout the exercise (scapular retraction).
4. Align the arms straight up from the shoulders, elbows slightly flexed and rotated out. Position the hands and dumbbells perpendicular to the body.

TECHNIQUE

1. Bend the elbows. Lower the arms to about 90 degrees from the body or parallel to the ground without rotating the shoulders.
2. Hold, then contract the chest. Pull the arms up and together to their original starting position without locking the elbows or rotating the shoulders.
3. Keep the chest tight at the finish of each repetition. Repeat.

BARBELL INCLINE CHEST PRESS

TARGET MUSCLES: Pectoralis major, anterior deltoid, triceps

JOINT MOTION: Horizontal adduction, elbow extension

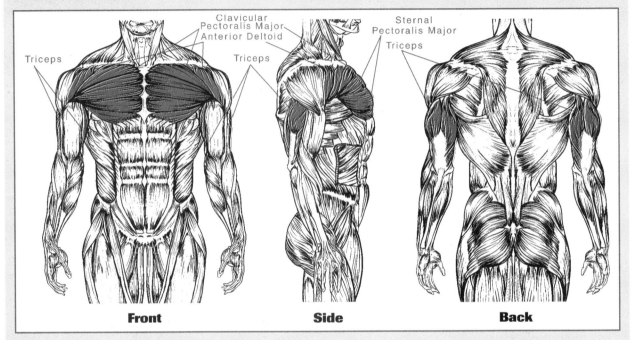

Front   **Side**   **Back**

EXERCISE DESCRIPTION

The Barbell Incline Chest Press is a two-joint motion exercise designed to target the upper chest and anterior deltoids, particularly the clavicular pectoralis major. The greater the incline becomes, the less the sternal pectoralis fibers are able to assist and the more the clavicular pectoralis and anterior deltoid fibers are targeted. The incline can be increased to a point that the anterior deltoid becomes the main target muscle. Then the exercise is referred to as a barbell front delt press.

EXERCISE TIPS

- Keep the feet planted flat and the head and sacrum pressed firmly against the bench.
- Avoid lowering the arms any deeper than parallel to the floor.
- Avoid rotating the shoulders or bending the wrists.
- Keep the shoulder blades together and a natural arch in the lower back throughout the exercise.

BARBELL INCLINE CHEST PRESS

ALIGNMENT AND POSITIONING

1. Plant the feet firmly onto the floor or an elevated platform.
2. Place the sacrum, head, and shoulder blades firmly onto the bench, keeping a natural arch in the lower back.
3. Pull the shoulder blades firmly together, and hold them there throughout the exercise (scapular retraction).
4. Place the hands outside the shoulders, forming approximately a 90-degree angle at the elbows when the upper arms are parallel to the floor.

TECHNIQUE

1. Bend the elbows. Lower the arms until they form about a 90-degree angle or when the upper arms are parallel to the ground.
2. Hold, then contract the chest. Pull the arms up and together to their original starting position without locking the elbows or rotating the shoulders.
3. Keep the chest tight at the finish of each repetition. Repeat.

DUMBBELL CHEST ADDUCTION

TARGET MUSCLES: Pectoralis major, anterior deltoid

JOINT MOTION: Horizontal adduction

Front   Side   Back

EXERCISE DESCRIPTION

A Dumbbell Chest Adduction is a single-joint motion exercise designed to isolate the chest muscles, particularly the sternal pectoralis major. If using lighter weight loads, this exercise can be a good way to learn how the chest functions by performing the specific joint motion for which it is responsible. However, the stressful forces placed on the shoulder joint when the arm is out away from the body and holding on to a free weight makes this exercise difficult and possibly dangerous to do with heavy resistance. Progress to a cable machine if you are ready to increase the intensity of this exercise or switch to a dumbbell chest press if continuing to use free weights.

EXERCISE TIPS

- Keep the feet planted flat and the head and sacrum pressed firmly against the bench.
- Avoid lowering the arms any deeper than when they are parallel to the floor.
- Avoid rotating the elbows or shoulders.
- Keep the shoulder blades together and a natural arch in the lower back throughout the exercise.

DUMBBELL CHEST ADDUCTION

ALIGNMENT AND POSITIONING

1. Plant the feet firmly onto the floor or an elevated platform.

2. Place the sacrum, head, and shoulder blades firmly onto the bench, keeping a natural arch in the lower back.

3. Pull the shoulder blades tightly together, and hold them there throughout the exercise (scapular retraction).

4. Align the arms straight up from the shoulders, elbows slightly flexed and rotated out. Position the hands and dumbbells perpendicular to the body (or parallel if using heavier weight).

TECHNIQUE

1. Lower the arms down to about 90 degrees from the body or parallel to the ground. Keep the elbows slightly bent, and do not rotate the shoulders.

2. Hold, then contract the chest, and pull the arms up and together to their original starting position without extending the elbows or rotating the shoulders.

3. Keep the chest tight at the finish of each repetition. Repeat.

STANDING CABLE CHEST ADDUCTION

TARGET MUSCLES: Pectoralis major, anterior deltoid

JOINT MOTION: Horizontal adduction

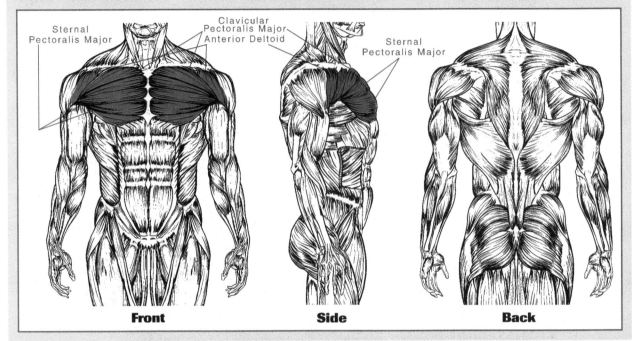

Front   Side   Back

EXERCISE DESCRIPTION

The Standing Cable Chest Adduction is a single-joint motion exercise designed to target the chest muscles, particularly the lower fibers of the sternal pectoralis major. Since the resistance is redirected overhead, the body needs to be aligned and positioned accordingly. This exercise may also be performed on a flat or inclined bench to target the middle or upper fibers of the chest, respectively.

EXERCISE TIPS

- Avoid rotating the shoulders after originally aligning them with the cables.
- Keep the arms from coming up any higher than about parallel to the floor.
- Keep the shoulder blades back, a natural arch in the lower back, and the head and neck in a neutral position throughout the exercise.

STANDING CABLE CHEST ADDUCTION

ALIGNMENT AND POSITIONING

1. Stand in front of the pulleys, centered between the cable columns. Be in a ready position, lightly grasping each handle.
2. Flex the hips. Bring the upper body over to about a 45- to 75-degree angle to the ground, keeping a natural arch in the lower back. (Upper-body angle will depend on your hamstring flexibility, lower-back stability, and which part of the chest you wish to target.)
3. Begin with the arms straight but not locked and the elbows pointed toward the pulleys.
4. Pull the shoulder blades in tightly together, and try to hold them there throughout the exercise (scapular retraction).

TECHNIQUE

1. Begin raising the arms out and up, keeping the elbows slightly bent and pointed toward the cables.
2. Keep a light grip on the handles and the wrists in neutral.
3. Continue to raise the arms out and up until they are about parallel to the ground.
4. Contract the chest. Pull the arms slowly back down to their original starting position without rotating the shoulders, locking the elbows, protracting the scapulae, or flexing the spine.
5. Hold and keep the chest tight. Repeat.

CABLE LAT EXTENSION

TARGET MUSCLES: Latissimus dorsi, teres major, posterior deltoid
(rhomboids, midtrapezius)

JOINT MOTION: Shoulder extension (partial scapular retraction)

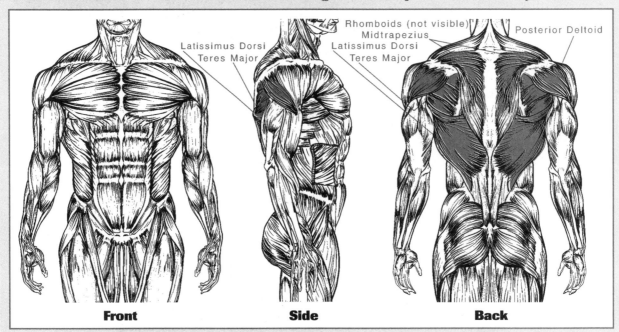

Front   Side   Back

EXERCISE DESCRIPTION

The Cable Lat Extension is a single-joint motion exercise designed to target the muscles of the back, particularly the latissimus dorsi. A partial scapular retraction is also performed during this exercise, which recruits the rhomboids and the midtrapezius as well. This exercise can be performed on the lat pull down machine or on an overhead cable machine. Since this is a single-joint motion, less weight will be used than in the lat pull down.

EXERCISE TIPS

- Keep the elbows slightly bent and pointed to the outside.
- Keep the wrists in neutral and the hands relaxed.
- Keep the shoulder blades down and together, a natural arch in the lower back, and the head and neck in a neutral position throughout the exercise.

CABLE LAT EXTENSION

ALIGNMENT AND POSITIONING

1. Stand in a ready position, arm's length from the bar of the lat pull down or overhead cable machine.

2. Slightly bend the knees and hips, pull the shoulders back, and create a natural arch in the lower back.

3. Place the hands lightly on top of the bar just outside shoulder width.

4. Begin with the elbows pointed out, slightly bent, and the arms approximately parallel to the floor (or higher as long as tension can be maintained in the lats).

TECHNIQUE

1. Contract the lats, and begin pulling the arms down and back toward the body.

2. Keep the elbows rotated out and slightly bent, with the wrists neutral and hands relaxed.

3. Continue to pull the arms down and back as far as you can while keeping the shoulder blades down and together and a natural arch in the lower back.

4. Hold, then slowly let the arms return to their original starting position, keeping tension in the lats. Repeat.

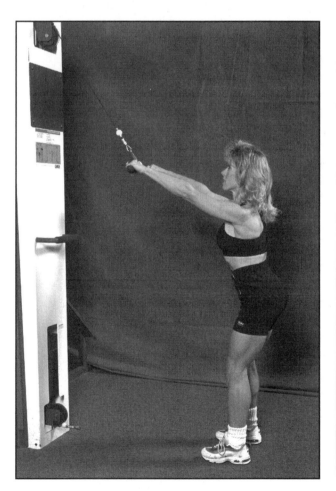

CABLE SEATED LAT ROW

TARGET MUSCLES: Rhomboids, midtrapezius, latissimus dorsi, teres major, posterior deltoid, biceps group

JOINT MOTION: Scapular retraction, shoulder extension, elbow flexion

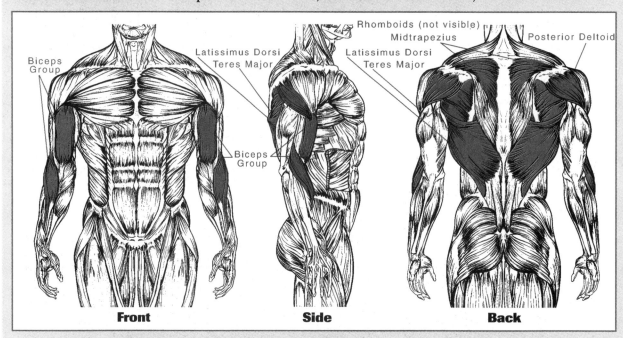

Front   **Side**   **Back**

EXERCISE DESCRIPTION

The Cable Seated Lat Row is a multiple-joint motion exercise designed to target the muscles of the middle back, particularly the latissimus dorsi, midtrapezius, and rhomboids. When done correctly, the entire ready position of the spine is directly resisted, making this an excellent exercise for all of the muscles necessary for good posture. Therefore, this exercise can be an important part of a person's base program since being able to hold the body in positions with good posture is required for so many other exercises. Several seated lat row machines can be used or substituted for the cable seated lat row machine, but the technique will be the same.

EXERCISE TIPS

- Keep the elbows pointed down. Avoid rotating the shoulders during the exercise.
- Keep the hands and arms as relaxed as possible, and concentrate on pulling with the back muscles.
- Keep the shoulder blades together and down, a natural arch in the lower back, and the head and neck in a neutral position.

CABLE SEATED LAT ROW

ALIGNMENT AND POSITIONING

1. Plant the feet firmly onto the floor or against the machine.

2. Sit up in a ready position with the hips and knees flexed. Create a natural arch in the lower back.

3. Lightly hold a set of pulley handles, keeping the wrists in a neutral position and the elbows slightly bent and pointed down.

TECHNIQUE

1. Keeping the arms just slightly bent, contract the rhomboids, and pull the shoulder blades together and down (scapular retraction). (This joint motion can be held during the entire exercise, done at the beginning of each rep, or performed separately to target the rhomboids and midtrapezius.)

2. Continue to squeeze the shoulder blades together. Contract the lats. Pull the arms back, keeping them close to the side of the body until the elbows are about straight down from the shoulders.

3. Hold, and contract the rhomboids, midtrapezius, and lats. Maintain a natural arch in the lower back, and keep the arms as relaxed as possible.

4. Slowly return the arms and lats back to the original start position, keeping the scapulae retracted (or released after each rep if desired) and tension in the lats. Repeat.

CABLE STANDING LAT ROW

TARGET MUSCLES: Rhomboids, midtrapezius, latissimus dorsi, posterior deltoid, biceps group

JOINT MOTION: Scapular retraction, shoulder extension, elbow flexion

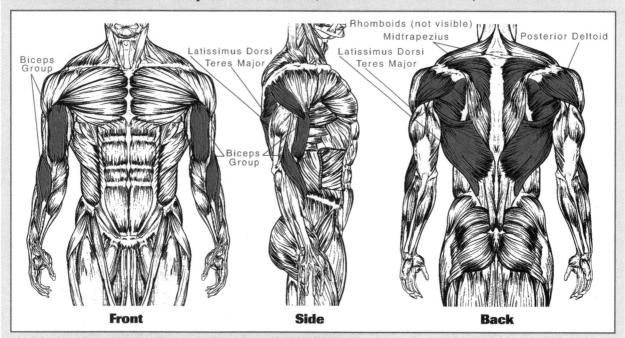

Front   Side   Back

EXERCISE DESCRIPTION

The Cable Standing Lat Row is a multiple-joint motion exercise designed to target the muscles of the middle back, particularly the latissimus dorsi, midtrapezius, and rhomboids. Much like the seated version of this exercise, the cable standing lat row trains all the muscles necessary to develop and maintain good posture. However, due to the standing position, this exercise places more demand on the legs, hips, and lower back. This demand makes the cable standing lat row a more challenging exercise and also a more functional exercise for learning how to pick up objects in everyday life than the seated version. This exercise can be performed in a similar fashion with dumbbells or with a T-bar row.

EXERCISE TIPS

- Keep the elbows pointed down. Avoid rotating the shoulders during the exercise.
- Keep the hands and arms as relaxed as possible, and concentrate on pulling with the back muscles.
- Keep the shoulder blades together and down, a natural arch in the lower back, and the head and neck in a neutral position.

CABLE STANDING LAT ROW

ALIGNMENT AND POSITIONING

1. Stand in a ready position with the feet spread just outside shoulder width.
2. With wrists in neutral, grasp a set of pulley handles with a loose grip.
3. Bend at the hips and slightly at the knees, fixing the trunk at about a 45-degree angle from the floor. Have the back in a ready position and the body's weight over the ankles.
4. Keep the elbows pointed down and slightly bent.

TECHNIQUE

1. Keeping the arms just slightly bent, contract the rhomboids and pull the shoulder blades together and down (scapular retraction).
2. Continue to squeeze the shoulder blades together, contract the lats, and pull the arms back. Keep the arms close to the side of the body until the elbows are about straight down from the shoulders.
3. Hold and contract the rhomboids, midtrapezius, and lats, maintaining a natural arch in the lower back and keeping the arms as relaxed as possible.
4. Slowly return the arms and the lats to the original start position, keeping the scapulae retracted and tension in the lats. Repeat.

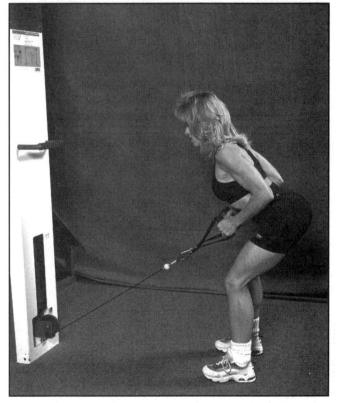

DUMBBELL ONE ARM LAT ROW

TARGET MUSCLES: Latissimus dorsi, teres major, rhomboids, midtrapezius, posterior deltoid, biceps group

JOINT MOTION: Scapular retraction, shoulder extension, elbow flexion

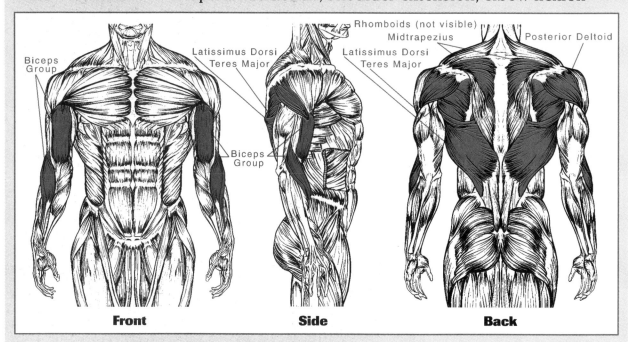

Front   Side   Back

EXERCISE DESCRIPTION

The Dumbbell One Arm Lat Row is a multiple-joint motion exercise designed to work the muscles of the back, particularly the latissimus dorsi, midtrapezius, and rhomboids. Using one arm at a time allows you to focus on one side of the back while using the other arm to provide stabilization. This exercise can be done using a cable machine as well, which will change the direction of the resistance. The dumbbell one arm lat row can be performed either in a standing position as shown or by bracing one knee on a bench as long as spinal positioning is maintained.

EXERCISE TIPS

- Avoid rotating the shoulders during the exercise.
- Keep the hands and arms as relaxed as possible, and concentrate on pulling with the back muscles.
- Keep the shoulder blades together and down, a natural arch in the lower back, and the head and neck in a neutral position.

DUMBBELL ONE ARM LAT ROW

ALIGNMENT AND POSITIONING

1. Stand in a ready position with the feet spread just outside shoulder width, or place one knee onto a bench so that the knees are at an equal height.

2. Bend the hips and knees. Plant one hand onto a bench so that the trunk is at an approximate 45- to 90-degree angle to the floor with the spine in a ready position.

3. Lightly hold the dumbbell with the arm pointing straight down. Keep the wrist in neutral, and the elbow slightly bent.

4. Keep the elbow of the stationary arm slightly bent, the shoulder blades back, and the head in a neutral position.

TECHNIQUE

1. Begin pulling the arm up with the elbow pointing straight back and close to the side of the body.

2. Continue to pull the arm back and up until the upper arm is about parallel to the floor.

3. Hold, and contract the rhomboids, midtrapezius, and lats. Maintain a natural arch in the lower back, and keep the arm as relaxed as possible.

4. Slowly return the arm and lats back to the original start position, keeping the scapulae retracted and tension in the lats. Repeat.

CABLE OVERHEAD LAT ROW

TARGET MUSCLES: Rhomboids, midtrapezius, latissimus dorsi, posterior deltoid, biceps group

JOINT MOTION: Scapular retraction, shoulder extension, elbow flexion

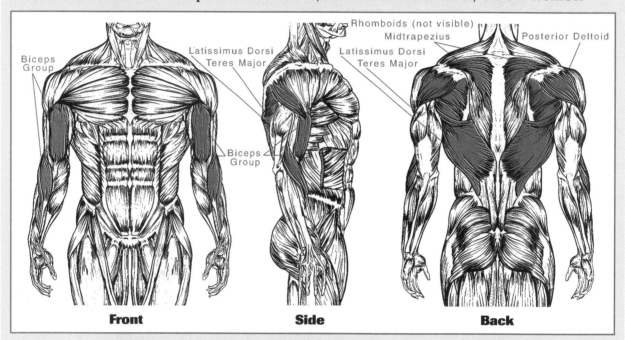

Front   **Side**   **Back**

EXERCISE DESCRIPTION

The Cable Overhead Lat Row is a multiple-joint motion exercise designed to target the muscles of the middle back, particularly the latissimus dorsi, midtrapezius, and rhomboids. The cable overhead lat row is a lot like the seated version of this exercise, because it trains all the muscles necessary to develop and maintain good posture. However, in this exercise, the resistance now comes from an overhead angle. Progress to this exercise after the lower angle has first been mastered and the shoulder joints have been strengthened and stabilized. This exercise is, however, much easier on the shoulder joints than a lat pull down or pull up, so it may serve as an intermediate stage in progressing to overhead motions.

EXERCISE TIPS

- Keep the elbows pointed down. Avoid rotating the shoulders during the exercise.
- Keep the hands and arms as relaxed as possible, and concentrate on pulling with the back muscles.
- Keep the shoulder blades together and down, a natural arch in the lower back, and the head and neck in a neutral position.

CABLE OVERHEAD LAT ROW

ALIGNMENT AND POSITIONING

1. Plant the feet firmly onto the floor and keep the knees braced under the pad.
2. Sit up in a ready position with a slight backward lean, and create a natural arch in the lower back.
3. Lightly hold a set of pulley handles, the wrists in a neutral position, and the elbows slightly bent and pointed down.

TECHNIQUE

1. Keeping the arms just slightly bent, contract the rhomboids and lower the traps to pull the shoulder blades down and together.
2. Continue to squeeze the shoulder blades together, contract the lats, and pull the arms down until they form about a 90-degree angle, keeping them close to the side of the body.
3. Hold and contract the rhomboids, midtrapezius, and lats, maintaining a natural arch in the lower back and keeping the arms as relaxed as possible.
4. Slowly return the arms back to the original start position, keeping the scapulae down and tension in the lats. Repeat.

CABLE LAT PULL DOWN

TARGET MUSCLES: Latissimus dorsi, teres major, posterior deltoid, rhomboids, middle and lower trapezius, levator scapulae, biceps groups

JOINT MOTION: Combination of shoulder adduction and horizontal shoulder abduction, scapular downward rotation, elbow flexion (assisting scapular depression and scapular retraction)

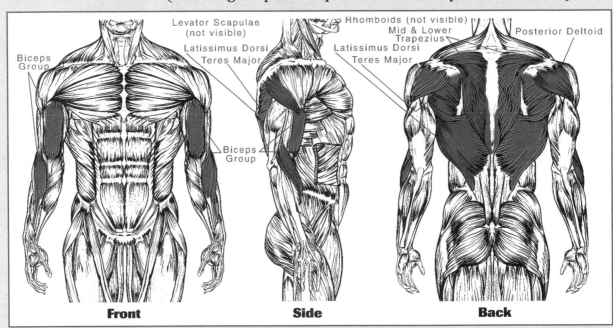

Front   Side   Back

EXERCISE DESCRIPTION

The Cable Lat Pull Down is primarily a two-joint motion exercise designed to target the latissimus dorsi muscles. However, other muscles of the back such as the lower and midtrapezius, rhomboids, and erector spinae are worked as well. Since the muscle fibers of the lats originate from the spine at a variety of angles before inserting into the upper arm, alignment to the resistance can also be set at a variety of angles by leaning back anywhere from about 15 to 45 degrees. Sitting straight up or vertically does not align the muscles with the resistance as efficiently. Pulling the bar behind the head can be stressful on the shoulder joints and is not advised.

EXERCISE TIPS

- Keep the elbows and forearms in direct line with the cable. Avoid rotating the shoulder during the exercise.
- Keep the hands and arms as relaxed as possible, and concentrate on pulling with the back muscles.
- Keep the shoulder blades down and together, a natural arch in the lower back, and the head and neck in a neutral position.

CABLE LAT PULL DOWN

ALIGNMENT AND POSITIONING

1. Place the hands onto the bar so that when the upper arms are parallel to the floor, they will form an approximate 90-degree angle with the forearms.

2. Sit with the knees under the pad, and lean back somewhere between 15 to 45 degrees.

3. Hold the bar with the arms slightly bent and the elbows pointed out.

4. Pull the shoulder blades down and together, and create a natural arch in the lower back.

TECHNIQUE

1. Contract the lats, bend the elbows, and begin to pull the arms out and down until the upper arms are about parallel to the floor (or slightly lower if you're able to keep the shoulder blades down and the forearms in line with the cable).

2. Keep the scapulae depressed and retracted, the spine stabilized, and a natural arch in the lower back.

3. Hold, continue to contract the lats, and relax the hands and arms as much as possible.

4. Let the arms back up slowly to the original starting position keeping tension in the lats. Repeat.

LAT PULL UPS

TARGET MUSCLES: Latissimus dorsi, teres major, posterior deltoid, rhomboids, middle and lower trapezius, levator scapulae, biceps groups

JOINT MOTION: Shoulder adduction, scapular downward rotation, elbow flexion (assisting scapular depression and retraction)

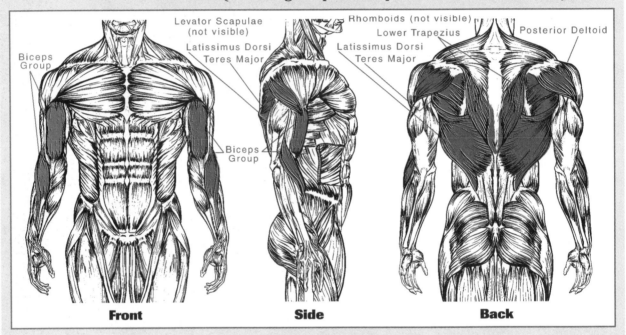

Front   Side   Back

EXERCISE DESCRIPTION

The Lat Pull Up is a two-joint motion exercise designed to work the muscles of the back, particularly the latissimus dorsi. Unlike the lat pull down, we are not able to redirect the resistance since the resistance is gravity. Therefore, aligning the muscles for the maximum efficiency becomes more difficult since the body is close to a vertical position. The lat pull up can be done on a machine that offers assistance of some sort or can be done free hanging if the individual is strong enough.

EXERCISE TIPS

- Keep the elbows pointed out, and avoid rotating the shoulders during the exercise.
- Keep the hands and arms as relaxed as possible, and concentrate on pulling with the back muscles.
- Keep the shoulder blades down and together, a natural arch in the lower back, and the head and neck in a neutral position.

LAT PULL UPS

ALIGNMENT AND POSITIONING

1. Place the hands on the bar so that when the upper arms are parallel to the floor, they will form an approximate 90-degree angle with the forearms.

2. Hang or stand on the support, and lean back slightly.

3. Hold the bar, keeping the arms slightly bent and the elbows pointed out.

4. Pull the shoulder blades down and together, and create a natural arch in the lower back.

TECHNIQUE

1. Contract the lats, and begin to pull the elbows out as the body rises.

2. Continue to pull the body up until the upper arms are about parallel to the floor. Keep the scapulae down and together and a natural arch in the lower back.

3. Hold, continue to contract the lats, and relax the hands and arms as much as possible.

4. Let the body back down slowly to the original starting position. Repeat.

DUMBBELL SCAPULAR ELEVATION

TARGET MUSCLES: Levator scapulae, upper trapezius, midtrapezius, rhomboids

JOINT MOTION: Scapular elevation (assisting scapular retraction and upward rotation)

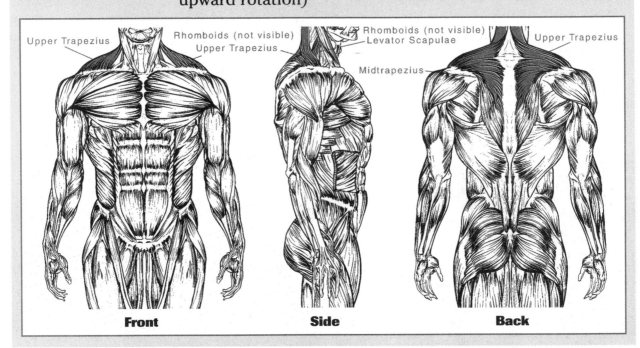

Front   Side   Back

EXERCISE DESCRIPTION

The Dumbbell Scapular Elevation is a single-joint motion exercise designed to target the levator scapulae and upper trapezius. A scapular retraction is set and held prior to performing the elevation. This aligns the pull of the targeted muscles against gravity.

EXERCISE TIPS

- Keep the shoulder blades together as you raise and lower them.
- Keep the arms relaxed but slightly bent.
- Lean forward, and keep weight on the heels.
- Maintain a natural arch in the lower back, and the neck and head in a neutral position.

DUMBBELL SCAPULAR ELEVATION

ALIGNMENT AND POSITIONING

1. Stand in a ready position with the arms hanging straight down. Hold the dumbbells, and keep the elbows slightly bent.
2. Bend at the hips and knees. Lean slightly forward while maintaining a natural arch in the lower back and keeping the weight over the ankles.
3. Pull the shoulder blades back and together, and hold them there (scapular retraction).

TECHNIQUE

1. Contract the levator scapulae and upper trapezius. Pull the arms straight up, bringing the shoulders behind the neck.
2. Hold and continue to contract the levator scapulae and upper trapezius, keeping the shoulder blades together.
3. Slowly lower the arms to the original start position. Repeat.

BARBELL SCAPULAR ELEVATION

TARGET MUSCLES: Levator scapulae, upper trapezius, midtrapezius, rhomboids

JOINT MOTION: Scapular elevation (assisting scapular retraction and upward rotation)

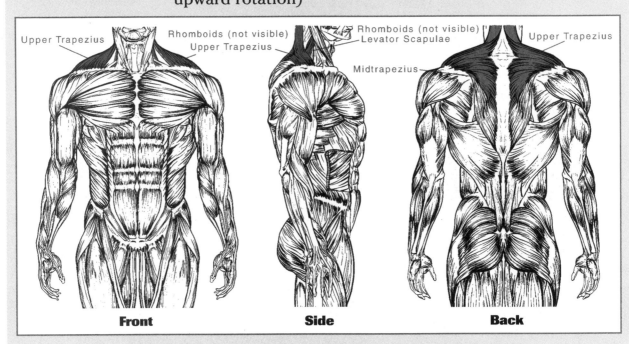

EXERCISE DESCRIPTION

The Barbell Scapular Elevation is a single-joint motion exercise designed to target the levator scapulae and upper trapezius. A scapular retraction is set and a forward lean is held prior to performing the elevation. This aligns the pull of the targeted muscles against gravity.

EXERCISE TIPS

- Keep the shoulder blades together as you raise and lower them.
- Keep the arms relaxed but slightly bent.
- Lean forward, and keep weight on the heels.
- Maintain a natural arch in the lower back, and the neck and head in a neutral position.

BARBELL SCAPULAR ELEVATION

ALIGNMENT AND POSITIONING

1. Stand in a ready position, hold a barbell, and keep the hands placed just outside shoulder width. (This hand positioning increases the amount of upward rotation.)

2. Bend at the hips and knees. Lean slightly forward while maintaining a natural arch in the lower back and keeping the weight over the ankles.

3. Pull the shoulder blades back and together, and hold them there (scapular retraction).

TECHNIQUE

1. Contract the levator scapulae and upper trapezius. Pull the arms straight up, bringing the shoulders behind the neck.

2. Hold, and continue to contract the levator scapulae and upper trapezius, keeping the shoulder blades together.

3. Slowly lower the arms to the original start position. Repeat.

MACHINE SCAPULAR DEPRESSION

TARGET MUSCLES: Lower trapezius, pectoralis minor, lower serratus anterior

JOINT MOTION: Scapular depression (assisting scapular retraction)

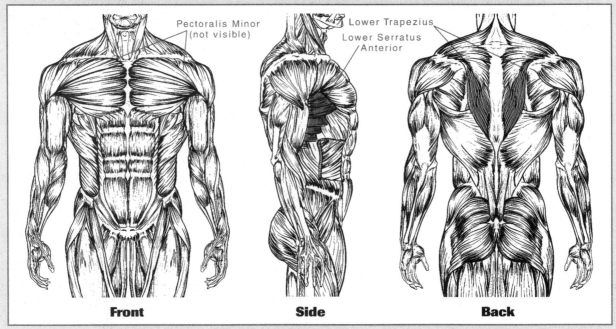

Front   Side   Back

EXERCISE DESCRIPTION

The Machine Scapular Depression is a single-joint motion exercise designed to target the pectoralis minor and lower serratus anterior. A scapular retraction is set and held in order to align the targeted muscles better against the resistance. This is a scapular exercise intended to balance and increase control of the scapular musculature. It strengthens the muscles that oppose elevation and that very rarely get challenged in most exercise programs or in everyday life.

EXERCISE TIPS

- Keep the shoulder blades together as you raise and lower them.
- Avoid twisting or rotating the shoulders. Keep the elbows pointed straight back and slightly bent.
- Keep a natural arch in the lower back, and the neck and head in a neutral position throughout the exercise.

MACHINE SCAPULAR DEPRESSION

ALIGNMENT AND POSITIONING

1. Sit on a triceps press machine. Plant the feet firmly onto the floor, and press the sacrum firmly against the pad.

2. Grasp the handles, keeping the wrists neutral and the elbows slightly flexed and pointed straight back.

3. Bend at the hips and lean forward while keeping a natural arch in the lower back.

4. Pull, and hold the shoulder blades tightly together (scapular retraction).

TECHNIQUE

1. Keeping the arms straight with the elbows slightly bent, slowly let the arms up while the shoulders come up behind the neck.

2. Contract the pectoralis minor, the lower traps, and the lower serratus anterior. Pull the arms and shoulder blades back down to the original start position.

3. Hold, continue to contract the scapular depressors. Repeat.

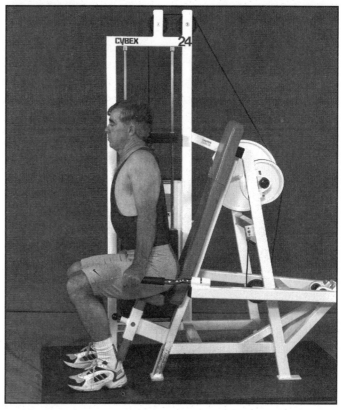

MACHINE SCAPULAR PROTRACTION

TARGET MUSCLES: Serratus anterior

JOINT MOTION: Scapular protraction

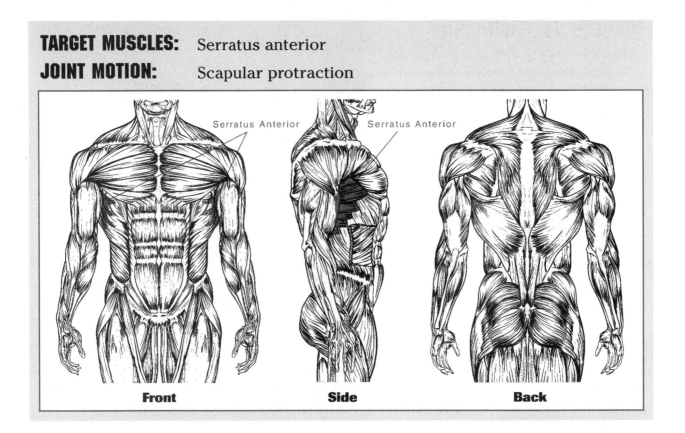

Serratus Anterior   Serratus Anterior

Front   **Side**   **Back**

EXERCISE DESCRIPTION

The Machine Scapular Protraction is a single-joint motion exercise designed to target the serratus anterior. This is a scapular exercise intended to balance and increase control of the scapular musculature by strengthening the muscles that oppose retraction. Protraction is involved in many normal, everyday activities, so it is usually not a motion that needs a lot of extra training. However, protraction may be part of a base program to increase scapular stabilization.

EXERCISE TIPS

- Avoid twisting or rotating the shoulders. Keep the elbows slightly bent.
- Keep a natural arch in the lower back, and the neck and head in a neutral position throughout the exercise.

MACHINE SCAPULAR PROTRACTION

ALIGNMENT AND POSITIONING

1. Sit on a chest press machine with the feet planted firmly on the machine. Press the sacrum and shoulder blades firmly against the pad (no retraction).

2. Position the spine in a ready position, keeping a natural arch in the lower back. Stabilize the head or lightly set it against the pad.

3. Grasp the handles. Have the arms straight, wrists in neutral, and elbows slightly bent.

TECHNIQUE

1. Contract the serratus anterior. Pull the arms and shoulder blades forward while keeping the head in place.

2. Hold, continue to contract the serratus anterior, and avoid locking the elbows.

3. Slowly bring the arms and shoulder blades back to their original starting position. Repeat.

CABLE SHOULDER INTERNAL ROTATION

TARGET MUSCLES: Subscapularis

JOINT MOTION: Shoulder internal rotation

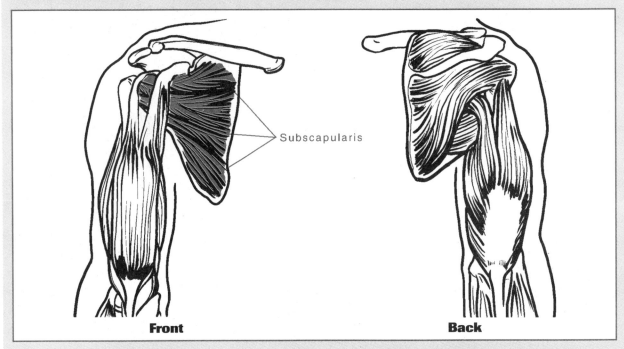

Subscapularis

Front   **Back**

EXERCISE DESCRIPTION

The Cable Shoulder Internal Rotation is a single-joint motion exercise designed to target the internal rotators of the shoulder, particularly the subscapularis. Rotator cuff exercises are an important part of any base program and should always be continued to provide good joint strength and stability.

EXERCISE TIPS

- Avoid twisting or rotating the trunk.
- Avoid externally rotating the shoulders farther than about 75 degrees.
- Keep the elbows pressed against the body or towel throughout the exercise.

CABLE SHOULDER INTERNAL ROTATION

ALIGNMENT AND POSITIONING

1. Stand in a ready position in front of and sideways to a cable machine.
2. Place a towel under the elbow, if needed, to align it slightly outside the shoulder.
3. Hold the pulley handle with the inside hand, keeping the arm at a 90-degree angle.
4. Press the arm tightly against the side of the body or towel, begin with the shoulder partially externally rotated (25 to 75 degrees, depending on shoulder stability and flexibility).

TECHNIQUE

1. Contract the internal rotator. Rotate the arm in front of and across the body as far as possible without the elbow lifting away from the side of the body or towel.
2. Hold and continue to contract the internal rotator, keeping the arm and hand relaxed.
3. Slowly return to the starting position. Repeat.

CABLE SHOULDER EXTERNAL ROTATION

TARGET MUSCLES: Infraspinatus, teres minor

JOINT MOTION: Shoulder external rotation

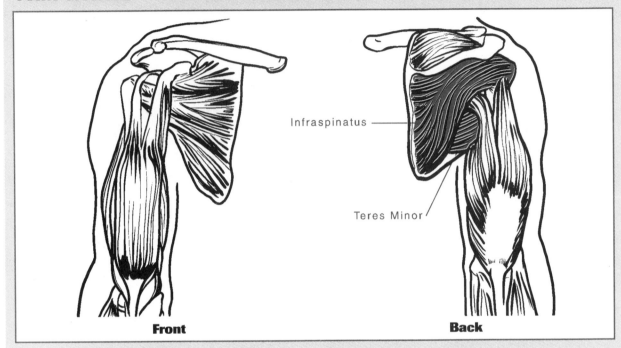

Infraspinatus

Teres Minor

Front   **Back**

EXERCISE DESCRIPTION

The Cable Shoulder External Rotation is a single-joint motion exercise designed to target the external rotators of the shoulder known as the infraspinatus and teres minor. Due to the large amount of muscles assisting with internal rotation, the importance of strengthening the external rotators is a key part of any base program. It should always be continued in order to provide good joint strength and shoulder stability.

EXERCISE TIPS

- Avoid twisting or any rotating of the trunk.
- Avoid externally rotating the shoulders farther than about 75 degrees.
- Keep the elbows pressed against the body or towel throughout the exercise.

CABLE SHOULDER EXTERNAL ROTATION

ALIGNMENT AND POSITIONING

1. Stand in a ready position in front of and sideways to a cable machine.
2. Place a towel under the elbow, if needed, to align it slightly outside the shoulder.
3. Hold the pulley handle, keeping the outside hand and arm at a 90-degree angle.
4. Press the arm tightly against the side of the body or towel. Begin with the shoulder slightly internally rotated while keeping the upper arm in place.

TECHNIQUE

1. Contract the external rotator and pull the arm across and out from the body as far as possible without the elbow lifting away from the side of the body or towel. Do not exceed 75 degrees of external rotation.
2. Hold and continue to contract the external rotator, keeping the arm and hand relaxed.
3. Slowly return to the starting position. Repeat.

DUMBBELL HORIZONTAL SHOULDER INTERNAL ROTATION

TARGET MUSCLES: Subscapularis

JOINT MOTION: Shoulder internal rotation

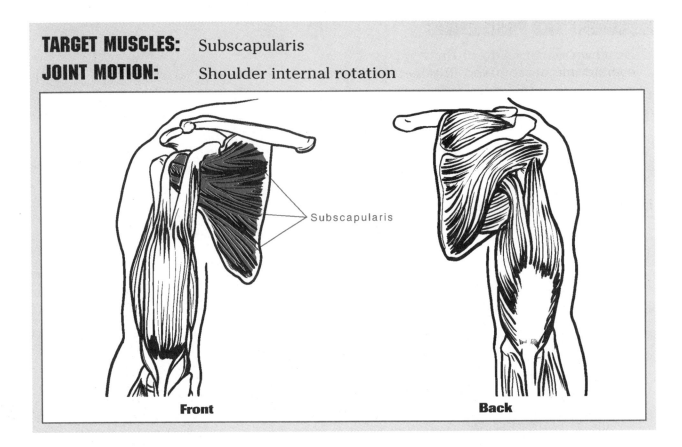

Subscapularis

Front   **Back**

EXERCISE DESCRIPTION

The Dumbbell Horizontal Shoulder Internal Rotation is a single-joint motion exercise designed to target the internal rotators of the shoulder, particularly the subscapularis. Rotator cuff exercises are an important part of any base program and should always be continued to provide good joint strength and stability.

EXERCISE TIPS

- Avoid twisting or rotating the trunk during the exercise.
- Keep the upper arm from sliding around as it rotates.
- Avoid rotating the arm up past the point of gravitational pull.
- Keep the head and neck in a neutral position.

DUMBBELL HORIZONTAL SHOULDER INTERNAL ROTATION

ALIGNMENT AND POSITIONING

1. Lie down on the side of the body in a comfortable and stable position, keeping a natural arch in the lower back.
2. Hold a dumbbell in the bottom hand, with the arm set in a 90-degree angle and horizontal from the body.
3. Hold the head and neck in a neutral position or brace them with a pad or towel.
4. Begin with the hand and dumbbell just off of the floor.

TECHNIQUE

1. Contract the internal rotators. Rotate the arm up as far as possible while still keeping a gravitational pull on the dumbbell.
2. Hold, continue to contract the internal rotators, and keep the arm and hand relaxed.
3. Slowly return to the starting position. Repeat.

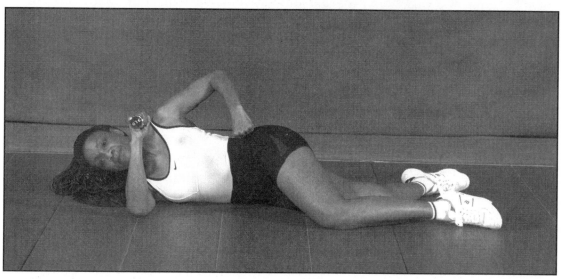

DUMBBELL SHOULDER EXTERNAL ROTATION

TARGET MUSCLES: Infraspinatus, teres minor

JOINT MOTION: Shoulder external rotation

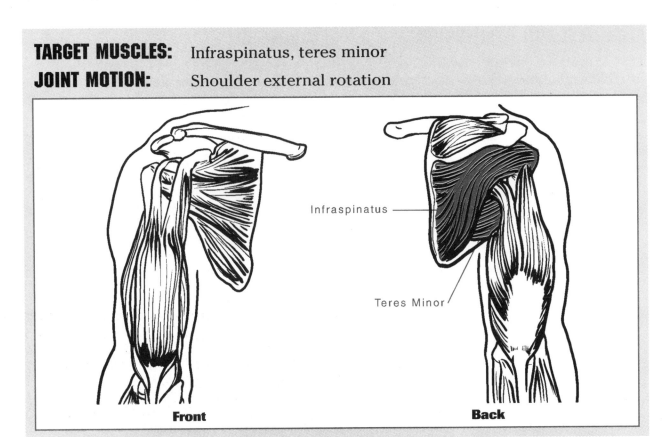

Infraspinatus

Teres Minor

Front   **Back**

EXERCISE DESCRIPTION

The Dumbbell Shoulder External Rotation is a single-joint motion exercise designed to target the external rotators of the shoulder known as the infraspinatus and teres minor. Due to the large amount of muscles assisting with internal rotation, the importance of strengthening the external rotators is a key part of any base program and should always be continued. This will provide good joint strength and shoulder stability.

EXERCISE TIPS

- Avoid twisting or rotating the trunk during the exercise.
- Avoid externally rotating the shoulder farther than about 75 degrees.
- Keep the elbow pressed against the body or towel throughout the exercise.
- Keep the head and neck in a neutral position throughout the exercise.

DUMBBELL SHOULDER EXTERNAL ROTATION

ALIGNMENT AND POSITIONING

1. Lie down on the side of the body in a comfortable and stable position, keeping the natural arch in the lower back.

2. Hold a dumbbell in the top hand and the arm in a 90-degree angle.

3. Place a towel under the elbow, if needed, to align it slightly higher than the level of the shoulder.

4. Press the arm tightly against the side of the body or towel, and begin with the shoulder slightly internally rotated.

5. Rest the bottom arm on the floor, or support the head if necessary.

TECHNIQUE

1. Contract the external rotators. Rotate the arm out and up from the body as far as possible without the elbow lifting away from the side of the body or exceeding 75 degrees of external rotation.

2. Hold, continue to contract the external rotators, and keep the arm and hand relaxed.

3. Slowly return to the starting position. Repeat.

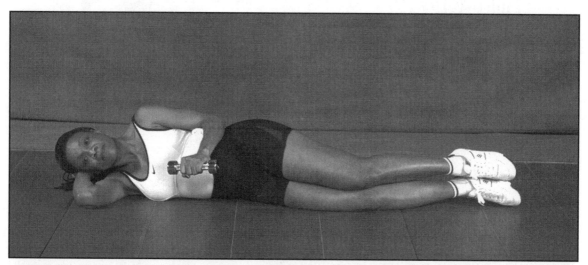

DUMBBELL HORIZONTAL SHOULDER EXTERNAL ROTATION

TARGET MUSCLES: Infraspinatus, teres minor

JOINT MOTION: Shoulder external rotation

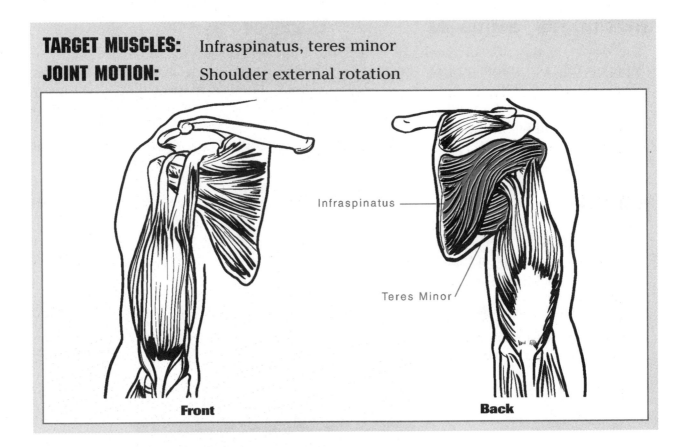

Front   Back

EXERCISE DESCRIPTION

The Dumbbell Horizontal Shoulder External Rotation is a single-joint motion exercise designed to target the external rotators of the shoulder known as the infraspinatus and teres minor. Due to the large amount of muscles assisting with internal rotation, strengthening the external rotators is an important part of any base program. It should always be continued to provide good joint strength and shoulder stability. This exercise can be done with one arm or with both arms at the same time. The upper arms however must be braced to properly target the external rotators.

EXERCISE TIPS

- Maintain a natural arch in the lower back, and avoid twisting or rotating the trunk during the exercise.
- Avoid letting the lower arm rotate below an angle parallel to the floor.
- Avoid externally rotating the shoulder past 90 degrees.
- Keep the elbow lightly pressed against the support throughout the exercise.

▌DUMBBELL HORIZONTAL SHOULDER EXTERNAL ROTATION

ALIGNMENT AND POSITIONING

1. Sit on a chair or bench in a ready position.
2. Brace the arms in a position parallel to the floor with the elbows slightly in front of and below the shoulders.
3. Begin with the arms level and bent at a 90-degree angle.

TECHNIQUE

1. Contract the external rotators. Rotate the arms up as far as possible without the elbows lifting off of their support and without exceeding the point where there is no gravitational pull on the dumbbells.
2. Hold, continue to contract the external rotators, and have the arms and hands relaxed.
3. Slowly return to the starting position. Repeat.

DUMBBELL FRONT DELT FLEX

TARGET MUSCLES: Anterior deltoid, clavicular pectoralis major, coracobrachialis

JOINT MOTION: Shoulder flexion

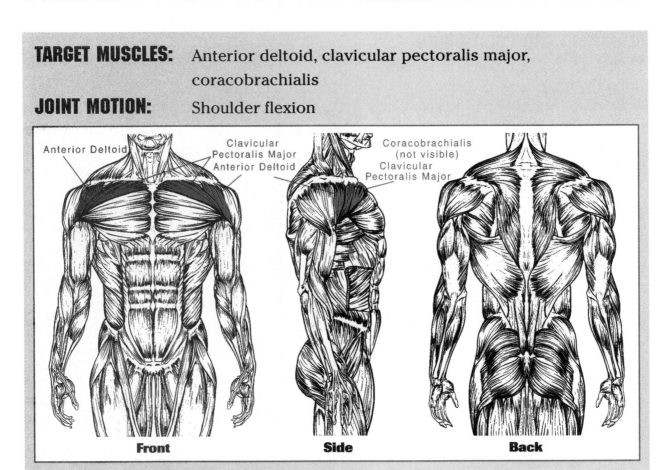

Front   Side   Back

EXERCISE DESCRIPTION

The Dumbbell Front Delt Flex (also known as a front delt raise) is a single-joint motion exercise designed to target the shoulder flexors, particularly the anterior deltoids. The positioning of the shoulders as they flex is important for efficiently challenging the anterior portion of the deltoids and for ensuring the safety of the joints. Keep the weight light due to the potential negative forces placed upon the shoulder joint. Switch to a front delt or incline chest press if you wish to challenge these muscles with heavier weight loads.

EXERCISE TIPS

- Avoid any twisting or rotating of the shoulders during the exercise.
- Keep the elbows pointed down and slightly bent.
- Keep the shoulder blades back and down, a natural arch in the lower back, and the head and neck in a neutral position throughout the exercise.

DUMBBELL FRONT DELT FLEX

ALIGNMENT AND POSITIONING

1. Stand in a ready position with the feet about shoulder-width apart and the knees and hips slightly bent.
2. Hold the dumbbells parallel to the body, shoulders and wrists in neutral, with the elbows pointing back and slightly bent.
3. Begin with the arms forward and up enough so that there is some degree of gravitational pull on the dumbbells providing a resistance.

TECHNIQUE

1. Contract the anterior deltoids. Begin pulling the arms up and slightly out, keeping the hands relaxed and the elbows slightly bent.
2. Pull the arms up and out until they are approximately parallel to the floor. Keep the hands in neutral and just outside shoulder width.
3. Hold and continue to contract the anterior deltoids. Have the arms relaxed, the elbows pointed down, and the wrists in a neutral position.
4. Slowly lower the arms back to their original start position. Repeat.

DUMBBELL SIDE DELT ABDUCTION

TARGET MUSCLES: Middle deltoid, anterior deltoid, supraspinatus

JOINT MOTION: Shoulder abduction

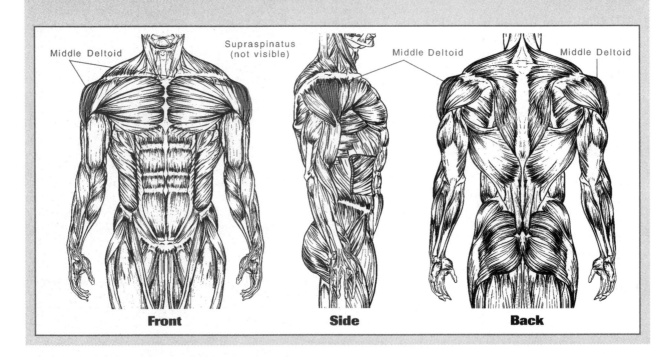

Middle Deltoid · Supraspinatus (not visible) · Middle Deltoid · Middle Deltoid

Front   **Side**   **Back**

EXERCISE DESCRIPTION

The Dumbbell Side Delt Abduction (also known as a side delt raise) is a single-joint motion exercise designed to target shoulder abductors, particularly the middle deltoids. The positioning of the shoulders as they abduct is important for effectively challenging the middle fibers of the deltoids and for ensuring the safety of the joints. Due to the stressful forces placed on the shoulder joints with the arms away from the body and holding free weights, I suggest keeping the weight loads light and using a cable machine or variable resistance machine if you feel you need to increase the intensity. Keep in mind that the shoulder is not designed to be exceptionally strong in abduction.

EXERCISE TIPS

- Avoid any twisting or rotating of the shoulders during the exercise.
- Keep the elbows pointed back and slightly bent.
- Lean forward, and keep weight over the ankles.
- Keep the shoulder blades together and down, a natural arch in the lower back, and the head and neck in a neutral position throughout the exercise.

DUMBBELL SIDE DELT ABDUCTION

ALIGNMENT AND POSITIONING

1. Stand in a ready position with the feet about shoulder-width apart and the knees and hips slightly bent.

2. Lean forward to align the middle fibers of the deltoids with gravity and to keep the weight over the ankles.

3. Place the arms straight down with the shoulders and wrists in neutral, and the elbows pointing back and slightly bent.

4. Begin with the arms out to the side far enough so that there is some degree of gravitational pull on the dumbbells, providing a resistance.

TECHNIQUE

1. Contract the middle deltoids. Begin pulling the arms out and up, keeping the hands relaxed and the elbows slightly bent.

2. Pull the arms out until they are approximately parallel to the floor with the hands just in front of the shoulders.

3. Hold and continue to contract the deltoids with the arms relaxed, the elbows pointed back, and the wrists in a neutral position.

4. Slowly lower the arms back to their original start position, keeping tension on the middle deltoids. Repeat.

DUMBBELL REAR DELT ROW

TARGET MUSCLES: Posterior deltoid, upper trapezius, midtrapezius, rhomboids, biceps group

JOINT MOTION: Shoulder horizontal abduction, scapular retraction, elbow flexion

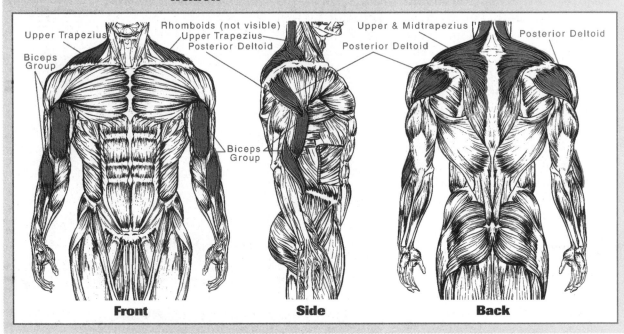

Front　　　　　　Side　　　　　　Back

EXERCISE DESCRIPTION

The Dumbbell Rear Delt Row is a two-joint motion exercise designed to target the shoulder horizontal abductors, particularly the posterior deltoids. A scapular retraction is first set in order to enable the shoulder joints to move more smoothly and safely. This also increases the optimum range of motion. Being able to hold the body in a position where the posterior deltoids are aligned against gravity is very difficult and may not be appropriate for some people, depending on their hamstring flexibility and lower-back stability. Alternative exercises are presented that can be substituted for or done prior to progressing to this one. The positioning of the shoulders for this exercise is important for effectively challenging the posterior portion of the deltoids and for ensuring the safety of the joints.

EXERCISE TIPS

- Avoid any twisting or rotating of the shoulders or trunk during the exercise.
- Keep the elbows pointed out and up as they move.
- Lean forward, and keep weight over the ankles.
- Keep the shoulder blades together and down, a natural arch in the lower back, and the head and neck in a neutral position throughout the exercise.

DUMBBELL REAR DELT ROW

ALIGNMENT AND POSITIONING

1. Stand in a ready position with the feet just outside shoulder-width apart. Bend the knees and hips, and bring the trunk of the body between 45 and 75 degrees in relation to the floor. Keep a natural arch in the lower back and the weight over the ankles. (The degree of trunk flexion will depend on hamstring flexibility and lower-back stability.)

2. Hold the dumbbells perpendicular to the body, the arms straight down, and the elbows pointed out and slightly bent.

3. Pull and hold the shoulder blades tightly together throughout the exercise (scapular retraction).

4. Begin with the arms slightly out so that there is some degree of gravitational pull on the dumbbells, providing resistance.

TECHNIQUE

1. Contract the posterior deltoids. Begin bending the elbows and pulling the arms apart and up.

2. Pull the arms up and the elbows out until the upper arms are approximately parallel to the floor and form about a 90-degree angle.

3. Hold and continue to contract the posterior deltoids. Keep the arms relaxed, the elbows pointing up, and the scapulae retracted.

4. Slowly lower the arms back to their original start position, keeping the scapulae retracted and tension on the posterior delts. Repeat.

DUMBBELL BRACED REAR DELT ROW

TARGET MUSCLES: Posterior deltoid, upper trapezius, midtrapezius, rhomboids, biceps group

JOINT MOTION: Shoulder horizontal abduction, scapular retraction, elbow flexion

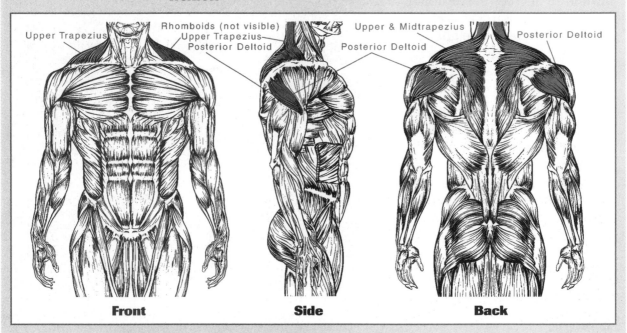

Upper Trapezius

Rhomboids (not visible)
Upper Trapezius
Posterior Deltoid

Upper & Midtrapezius
Posterior Deltoid

Posterior Deltoid

Front   **Side**   **Back**

EXERCISE DESCRIPTION

The Dumbbell Braced Rear Delt Row is a two-joint motion exercise designed to target the shoulder horizontal abductors, particularly the posterior deltoids. A scapular retraction is first set in order to enable the shoulder joints to move more smoothly and safely. This also increases the optimum range of motion. Using a bench to brace the body provides added stability and accommodates those individuals who have difficulty with the free standing version of this exercise. The positioning of the shoulders is important for effectively challenging the posterior portion of the deltoids and for ensuring the safety of the joints. Pay close attention to the directions.

EXERCISE TIPS

- Avoid any twisting or rotating of the shoulders during the exercise.
- Keep the elbows pointed out and up as they move.
- Keep the shoulder blades together and down, a natural arch in the lower back, and the head and neck in a neutral position throughout the exercise.

DUMBBELL BRACED REAR DELT ROW

ALIGNMENT AND POSITIONING

1. Sit or kneel in a ready position facing a bench. The bench should be set in order to align the trunk of the body between 45 and 90 degrees to the floor.

2. Hold the dumbbells perpendicular to the body. Keep the arms straight down and the elbows pointed out and slightly bent.

3. Pull and hold the shoulder blades tightly together throughout the exercise (scapular retraction).

4. Begin with the arms slightly out so that there is some degree of gravitational pull on the dumbbells, providing resistance.

TECHNIQUE

1. Contract the posterior deltoids. Begin bending the elbows and pulling the arms apart and up.

2. Pull the arms up and elbows out until the upper arms are approximately parallel to the floor and form about a 90-degree angle.

3. Hold, continue to contract the posterior deltoids. Keep the arms relaxed, the elbows pointing up, and the scapulae retracted.

4. Slowly lower the arms back to their original starting position, keeping the scapulae retracted and tension on the posterior deltoids. Repeat.

CABLE SEATED REAR DELT ROW

TARGET MUSCLES: Posterior deltoid, upper trapezius, midtrapezius, rhomboids, biceps group

JOINT MOTION: Shoulder horizontal abduction, scapular retraction, elbow flexion

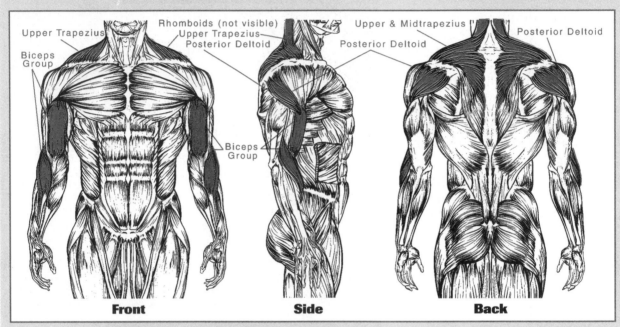

EXERCISE DESCRIPTION

The Cable Seated Rear Delt Row is a two-joint motion exercise designed to target the shoulder horizontal abductors, particularly the posterior deltoids. A scapular retraction is first set in order to enable the shoulder joints to move more smoothly and safely. This also increases the optimum range of motion. Sitting and using a cable machine requires more stabilization from the body and greater hamstring flexibility than using a type rowing machine that braces the upper body. The positioning of the shoulders for this exercise is important for effectively challenging the posterior portion of the deltoids and for ensuring the safety of the joints. Pay close attention to the directions.

EXERCISE TIPS

- Avoid any twisting or rotating of the shoulders or trunk during the exercise.
- Keep the elbows pointed out as they move.
- Keep the shoulder blades together and down, a natural arch in the lower back, and the head and neck in a neutral position throughout the exercise.

CABLE SEATED REAR DELT ROW

ALIGNMENT AND POSITIONING

1. Plant the feet firmly onto the floor or against the machine

2. Sit up in a ready position with the knees flexed, and create a natural arch in the lower back.

3. Lightly hold a set of pulley handles. Keep the wrists in a neutral position, the palms down, the arms aligned with the cable, and the elbows slightly bent and pointed out.

TECHNIQUE

1. Keep the arms just slightly bent, contract the rhomboids, and pull the shoulder blades together and down (scapular retraction).

2. Continue to squeeze the shoulder blades together. Contract the posterior deltoids. Pull the arms back and hands slightly apart, keeping them aligned with the cable until the elbows are almost straight out from the shoulders.

3. Hold, and contract the rhomboids, midtrapezius, and posterior deltoids. Maintain a natural arch in the lower back, and keep the arms as relaxed as possible.

4. Slowly return the arms back to the original starting position, keeping the scapulae retracted and tension on the posterior deltoids. Repeat.

CABLE STANDING REAR DELT ROW

TARGET MUSCLES: Posterior deltoid, upper trapezius, midtrapezius, rhomboids, biceps group

JOINT MOTION: Shoulder horizontal abduction, scapular retraction, elbow flexion

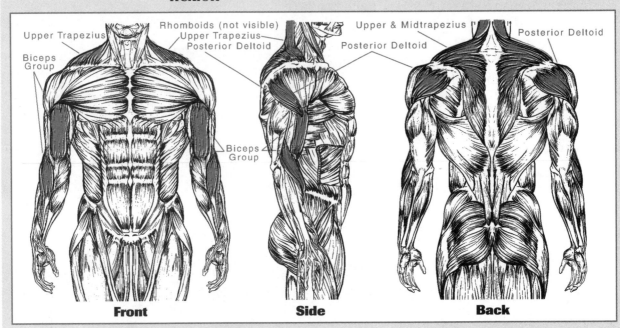

Front   Side   Back

EXERCISE DESCRIPTION

The Cable Standing Rear Delt Row is a two-joint motion exercise designed to target the shoulder horizontal abductors, particularly the posterior deltoids. A scapular retraction is first set in order to enable the shoulder joints to move more smoothly and safely. This also increases the optimum range of motion. Standing and using a cable machine requires more stabilization from the body than when performing a braced, seated version. Using the pulley handles also allows you to spread the hands apart as you pull back. This increases the efficiency of the exercise, which cannot be done on most machines. The positioning of the shoulders for this exercise is important for effectively challenging the posterior portion of the deltoids and for ensuring the safety of the joints.

EXERCISE TIPS

- Avoid any twisting or rotating of the shoulders or trunk during the exercise.
- Keep the elbows pointed out as they move.
- Keep the shoulder blades together and down, a natural arch in the lower back, and the head and neck in a neutral position throughout the exercise.

CABLE STANDING REAR DELT ROW

ALIGNMENT AND POSITIONING

1. Stand in a ready position with the feet set apart in front of and behind the body.
2. Bend the back knee, lean back, and create a natural arch in the lower back.
3. Raise the arms to align them directly with the cable. Keep the elbows slightly bent and pointed out.
4. Lightly hold onto a set of pulley handles, keeping the palms facing down.

TECHNIQUE

1. Keeping the arms just slightly bent, contract the rhomboids and pull the shoulder blades together and down (scapular retraction).
2. Continue to squeeze the shoulder blades together. Contract the posterior deltoids. Pull the arms back and the hands slightly apart, keeping them aligned with the cable until the elbows are almost straight out from the shoulders.
3. Hold, and contract the rhomboids, midtrapezius, and posterior deltoids. Maintain a natural arch in the lower back, and keep the arms as relaxed as possible.
4. Slowly return the arms back to the original starting position, keeping the scapulae retracted and tension in the posterior deltoids. Repeat.

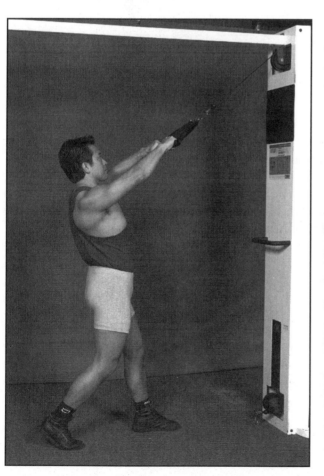
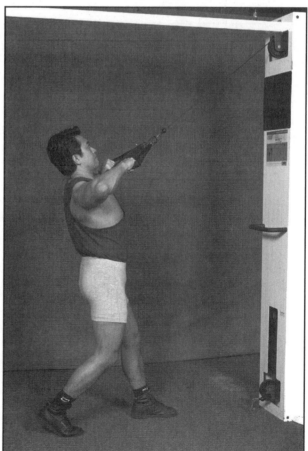

DUMBBELL BICEPS FLEX

TARGET MUSCLES: Biceps brachii, brachialis, brachioradialis

JOINT MOTION: Elbow flexion

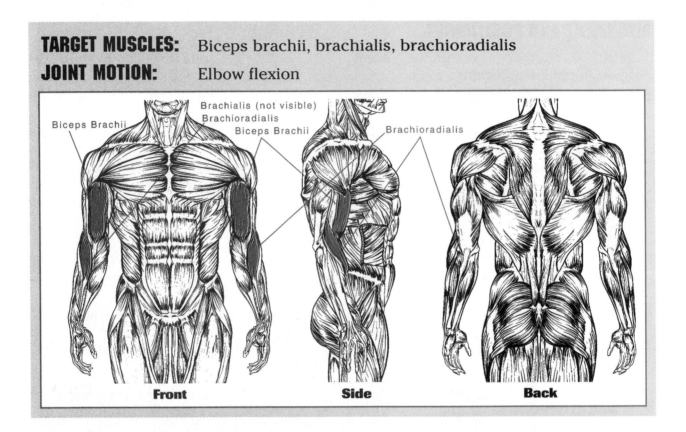

Front   Side   Back

EXERCISE DESCRIPTION

The Dumbbell Biceps Flex is a single-joint motion exercise designed to target the biceps muscle group. The portion of the biceps that is challenged the most depends on the positioning of the forearm and the rotation of the elbow. If the forearm is supinated and the palm is up, the biceps brachii is most active. When the forearm is in neutral or pronated the brachialis and brachioradialis become more active. Using dumbbells provides the opportunity to perform this exercise with any of these options. You can target whichever portion of the biceps group you desire by simply rotating the forearm prior to beginning the exercise.

EXERCISE TIPS

- Avoid any twisting or rotating of the shoulders or elbows during the exercise.
- Keep the elbows in place and slightly flexed at the start and finish of the exercise.
- Keep the shoulders back and down, a natural arch in the lower back, and the head and neck in a neutral position throughout the exercise.

DUMBBELL BICEPS FLEX

ALIGNMENT AND POSITIONING

1. Stand in a ready position with the feet about shoulder-width apart, the knees and hips slightly bent, and weight on the heels.

2. With the upper arms pulled firmly to the side of the body, hold the dumbbells with the lower arm supine, neutral, or partially pronated, depending on which portion of the biceps you wish to target.

3. Begin with the elbows aligned under the shoulders and slightly bent.

TECHNIQUE

1. Contract the biceps, flex the elbows, and with the hands relaxed, begin to pull the lower arms out and up in front of the body.

2. Pull the lower arms out and up in a natural angle from the elbow, as far as they will go, without moving the upper arms. Do not exceed the point of gravitational pull on the dumbbells.

3. Hold, relax the hands, and continue to contract the biceps.

4. Slowly lower the arms back to their original start position keeping tension on the biceps. Repeat.

BARBELL BICEPS FLEX

TARGET MUSCLES: Biceps brachii, brachialis, brachioradialis

JOINT MOTION: Elbow flexion

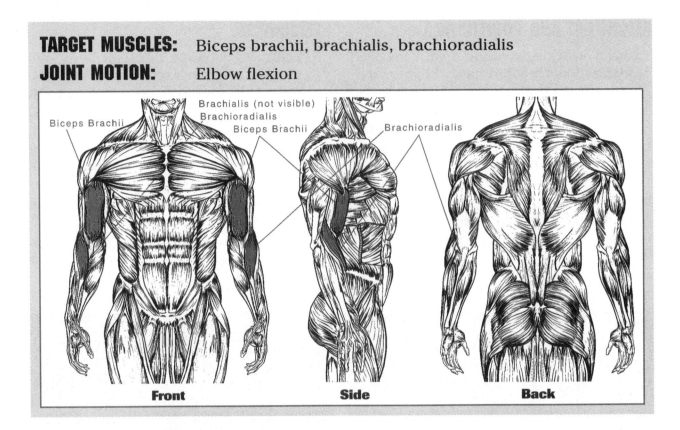

Front   Side   Back

EXERCISE DESCRIPTION

The Barbell Biceps Flex is a single-joint motion exercise designed to target the biceps muscle group. If using a straight bar, the lower arms are in a supinated position, which will recruit a maximum amount of muscle fibers of the biceps brachii. When using a barbell, be sure to have a grip that will accommodate the natural carrying angle of the elbow.

EXERCISE TIPS

- Avoid any twisting or rotating of the shoulders or elbows during the exercise.
- Keep the elbows in place and slightly flexed at the start and finish of the exercise.
- Keep the shoulders back and down, a natural arch in the lower back, and the head and neck in a neutral position throughout the exercise.

BARBELL BICEPS FLEX

ALIGNMENT AND POSITIONING

1. Stand in a ready position with the feet about shoulder-width apart, the knees and hips slightly bent, and weight on the heels.
2. With the upper arms pulled firmly to the side of the body, hold the barbell with the hands placed somewhere just outside shoulder width to allow for your natural carrying angle. (This angle varies in each person.)
3. Begin with the elbows aligned under the shoulders and slightly bent.

TECHNIQUE

1. Contract the biceps, flex the elbows, and with the hands relaxed, begin to pull the lower arms out and up in front of the body.
2. Pull the lower arms out and up in their natural angle from the elbows as far as they will go. Do not move the upper arms, and do not exceed the point of gravitational pull on the barbell.
3. Hold, relax the hands, and continue to contract the biceps.
4. Slowly lower the arms back to their original start position keeping tension on the biceps. Repeat.

CABLE BICEPS FLEX

TARGET MUSCLES: Biceps brachii, brachialis, brachioradialis

JOINT MOTION: Elbow flexion

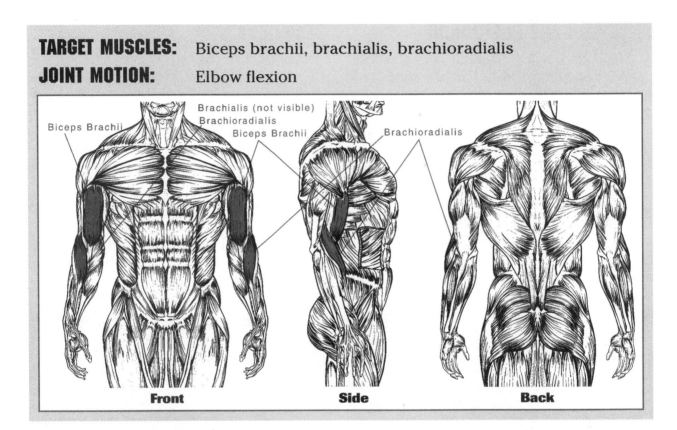

Front   Side   Back

EXERCISE DESCRIPTION

The Cable Biceps Flex is a single-joint motion exercise designed to target the biceps muscle group. Using a cable changes the direction of the resistance as compared with using free weights. Be sure to make the proper alignment adjustments with this in mind. If using a straight bar, the lower arms are in a supine position, which will recruit a maximum amount of the muscle fibers of the biceps brachii. When using a straight bar, be sure to have a grip that will accommodate the natural carrying angle of the elbow.

EXERCISE TIPS

- Avoid any twisting or rotating of the shoulders or elbows during the exercise.
- Keep the elbows slightly in front of the shoulders and slightly flexed at the start and finish of the exercise.
- Keep the shoulders back and down, a natural arch in the lower back, and the head and neck in a neutral position throughout the exercise.

CABLE BICEPS FLEX

ALIGNMENT AND POSITIONING

1. Stand in a ready position with the feet about shoulder-width apart, the knees and hips slightly bent, and weight on the heels.
2. With the upper arms pulled firmly to the side of the body, hold the bar with the hands placed somewhere just outside the shoulders to allow for your natural carrying angle. (This angle varies in each person.)
3. Begin with the elbows aligned just in front of the shoulders and slightly bent. Upper arms should be parallel to the cable.

TECHNIQUE

1. Contract the biceps, flex the elbows, and with the hands relaxed, begin to pull the lower arms out and up in front of the body.
2. Pull the lower arms out and up in their natural angle from the elbow as far as they go without moving the upper arms.
3. Hold, relax the hands, and continue to contract the biceps.
4. Slowly lower the arms back to their original start position. Repeat.

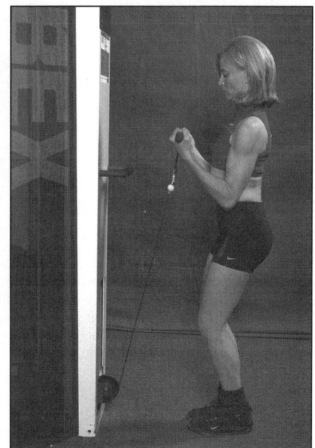

DUMBBELL TRICEPS EXTENSION

TARGET MUSCLES: Triceps long head, triceps medial head, triceps lateral head, anconeus

JOINT MOTION: Elbow extension

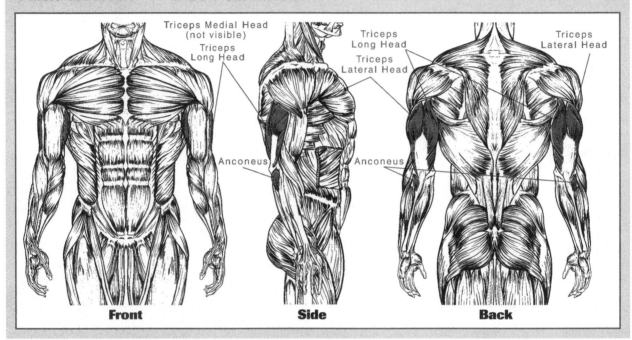

Front   Side   Back

EXERCISE DESCRIPTION

The Dumbbell Triceps Extension is a single-joint motion exercise designed to target the triceps muscle group. As opposed to the biceps, supinating or pronating the lower arm has very little effect on the triceps. Changing the focus of the resistance to a different portion of the triceps is accomplished instead by setting the shoulder in different degrees of flexion or extension. With this exercise, it is possible to preset the upper arm at different angles to shift the focus. The higher the degree of flexion, the more the muscle fibers of the triceps long head will be recruited and the less the triceps lateral head will assist.

EXERCISE TIPS

- Avoid twisting or rotating the shoulders or wrists during the exercise.
- Keep the elbows pointed toward the line of the body and avoid locking them.
- Avoid bringing the forearms lower than about a 90-degree angle.
- Keep the wrists neutral.
- Keep the shoulder blades down and together, a natural arch in the lower back, and the head and neck in a neutral position throughout the exercise.

DUMBBELL TRICEPS EXTENSION

ALIGNMENT AND POSITIONING

1. Plant the feet firmly onto the floor or an elevated platform.
2. Place the sacrum, shoulder blades, and head firmly against the bench. Maintain a natural arch in the lower back.
3. Set the arms straight up at approximately 90 degrees flexion with the elbows slightly bent and pointing toward the lower body.

TECHNIQUE

1. Slowly lower the forearms without moving the shoulders or upper arms.
2. Continue to lower the forearms, keeping them in line until they form an approximate 90-degree angle.
3. Hold, continue to contract the triceps, and slowly pull the lower arms back up to their original start position. Repeat.

CABLE TRICEPS EXTENSION

TARGET MUSCLES: Triceps long head, triceps medial head, triceps lateral head, anconeus

JOINT MOTION: Elbow extension

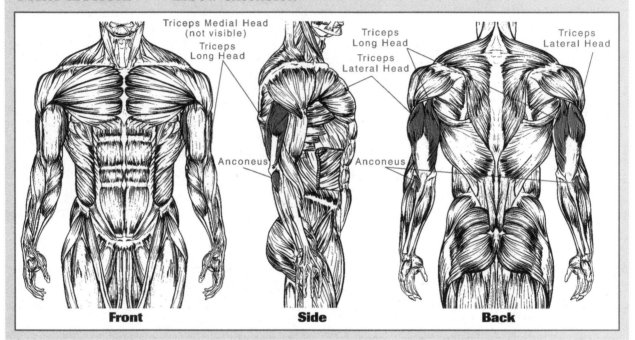

Triceps Medial Head (not visible)
Triceps Long Head
Anconeus
Triceps Long Head
Triceps Lateral Head
Anconeus
Triceps Lateral Head

Front   **Side**   **Back**

EXERCISE DESCRIPTION

The Cable Triceps Extension is a single-joint motion exercise designed to target the triceps muscle group, particularly the triceps lateral head. As opposed to the biceps, supinating or pronating the lower arms has very little effect on the triceps. Changing the focus of the resistance to a different portion of the triceps is accomplished by setting the shoulder in different degrees of flexion or extension and positioning the body at different angles to the machine. With this exercise, the shoulders are slightly extended to shift the focus toward the lateral head. As the degree of extension increases, less assistance is available to train the triceps long head so more recruitment comes from the muscle fibers of the triceps lateral head.

EXERCISE TIPS

- Avoid any movement of the shoulders and upper arms during the exercise.
- Avoid bringing the lower arms up to a point where there is a loss in the ability to control the arms or a loss of tension from the cable machine.
- Keep the wrists in a neutral position.
- Keep the shoulders back and together, a natural arch in the lower back, and the head and neck in a neutral position.

CABLE TRICEPS EXTENSION

ALIGNMENT AND POSITIONING

1. Stand in a ready position with the feet about shoulder-width apart.

2. Lean forward, keeping the weight over the ankles and a natural arch in the lower back.

3. Place the hands on top of the bar shoulder-width apart. Pull the elbows back to align the upper arms directly with the cable.

4. Begin with the elbows pointed back and tight against the side of the body.

TECHNIQUE

1. Slowly let the resistance pull the lower arms up and out in front of the body.

2. Continue to let the lower arms up to about a 90-degree angle while keeping the upper arms firmly in position.

3. Hold, relax the hands, and contract the triceps.

4. Keeping the upper arms in position, slowly pull the lower arms back to their original start position. Repeat.

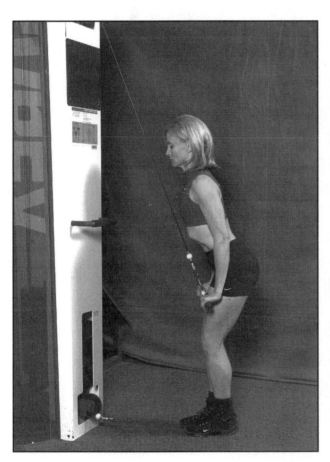

REFERENCES

Aaberg, E. 1996. *Bio-Mechanically Correct.* Dallas: R.I.P.T. Publishing.

Baechle, T., ed. 1994. *National Strength and Conditioning Manual.* Champaign, IL: Human Kinetics.

Blair, M. 1985. *A Spinal Specialist's Guide To Exercise, Fitness & Health.* Whitehall, VA: Better Way.

Calais-Germain, B. 1991. *Anatomy of Movement.* Seattle, WA: Eastland Press.

Fahey, T. 1994. *Weight Training for Men and Women,* 2nd ed. Mountain View, CA: Mayfield Publishing.

Fleck, S.J., and W.J. Kraemer. 1997. *Designing Resistance Training Programs,* 2nd ed. Champaign, IL: Human Kinetics.

Horrigan, J., and J. Robinson. 1991. *The 7 Minute Rotator Cuff Solution.* Los Angeles: Health For Life.

Howley, E.T., and B.D. Franks. 1997. *Health Fitness Instructors Handbook,* 3rd ed. Champaign, IL: Human Kinetics.

Jolly, R. (trans.) 1994. *The Color Atlas of Human Anatomy.* New York: Harmony Books.

Kreighbaum, E., and K.M. Barthels. 1985. *Biomechanics, A Qualitative Approach for Study of Human Movement,* 2nd. ed. Minneapolis, MN: Burgess.

Norkin, C., and P. Levangie. 1992. Joint Structure and Function, 2nd ed. Philadelphia: F.A. Davis Company.

Purvis, T., and M. Simmon. 1994. *Focus on Fitness Video Tape Series.* Oklahoma City: Focus on Fitness Productions.

Rasch, P.J., and Burke. 1978. *Kinesiology and Applied Anatomy,* 6th ed. Philadelphia: Lea & Febiger.

Stone, M.H., and H.S. O'Bryant. 1987. *Weight Training—A Scientific Approach.* Edina, MN: Burgess International.

Sudy, M., ed. 1991. *Personal Training Manual.* San Diego: American Council on Exercise.

INDEX

ABOUT THE AUTHOR

Everett Aaberg has been both a teacher and practitioner of resistance training for over 15 years. He is currently the Director of Education and Personal Training for International Athletic Club Management, Inc. in Dallas, Texas. Formerly the Education Coordinator and Senior Trainer at the world-renowned Cooper Fitness Center, he now serves as an instructor at the Cooper Institute for Aerobic Research for a specialty certification course entitled "The Biomechanics of Strength Training."

Aaberg holds a bachelor's degree in exercise science and recreation management with continuing education in exercise physiology, anatomy, kinesiology, biomechanics, and nutrition. He is a resistance training specialist and a certified personal trainer through some of the most highly accredited organizations in the United States—including the American Council on Exercise, the American College of Sports Medicine, and the National Academy of Sports Medicine. He's also a certified strength and conditioning specialist through the National Strength and Conditioning Association.

Aaberg has extensive practical experience in resistance training. He has instructed and trained thousands of athletes and fitness enthusiasts, coaches, fitness instructors, and personal trainers. Plus, he has personally used resistance training throughout his life for health and fitness as well as for preparation for a variety of sports and athletic competitions. Not only was he a collegiate Academic All-American in football, he has also won several state and national powerlifting championships and bodybuilding titles, including AAU and NPC Mr. Colorado titles and the Mr. Junior America title in his class. Aaberg lives and trains in Dallas, Texas.